What People Are Saying About

ROMANCE RECIPES

FOR THE

SOUL

"*Romance Recipes for the Soul* is an outstanding collection of powerful, heartwarming stories full of love and thoughtfulness."

– Marlene Wegner

"I'm giving this book to my husband!"

– Connie Forzano

"Finally, a man who knows what women want."

– Susan Arnold

"*Romance Recipes for the Soul* has helped me capture my girlfriend's heart."

– Ricky Baker

"The stories in this book really touched my heart. No other book or movie has ever done that before."

– Denice Janick

"I'm not the most sensitive guy in the world; however, some of these stories brought tears to my eyes. But don't tell anyone."

– Mike Meunier

"Be careful when simulating these dates; you may end up married."

– Jack Shrum

"My husband and I are always looking for special things to do on 'Date Night.' This book is the best!"

– Connie Messina

"This book has changed the way I plan dates."

– Joe Ferro

"Thanks for sharing such creative dating stories to help keep life exciting. *Romance Recipes for the Soul* is truly a blessing."

– Anna LoBello

"Frank Cabiroy is a genius."

– Ginny Hart

"You want to know a secret to a woman's heart? Buy this book."

– Karen Kennedy

"Funny, nostalgic, romantic—these stories spoke to my heart and warmed my soul."

– Lyn Wagner

ROMANCE
RECIPES
FOR THE
SOUL

MEN, WOMEN,
SINGLE OR MARRIED

*A*N
INSPIRING COLLECTION
OF ROMANTIC AND UNIQUE
REAL-LIFE DATING STORIES

FRANK CABIROY

Edited by Anne Walradt

PISCES PRESS PUBLISHING COMPANY
Virginia Beach, VA

Editor: Anne Walradt
Cover Designer: Tymm Smith

Published by Pisces Press Publishing Company

Requests for information should be addressed to:
Pisces Press Publishing Company
P.O. Box 3111
Virginia Beach, VA 23454

Phone: (757) 721-2184
Fax: (757) 721-7019
E-mail: PPPCo@aol.com
Web site: www.RomanceRecipes.com

ISBN: 1-888426-12-8

Dedication

I dedicate this book to my mentor, Salvatore,
President of Pisces Press Publishing Company.
Salvatore has always believed in me.
He is my inspiration.

Acknowledgments

*R*omance Recipes for the Soul is a true labor of love and romance for all of us, and I would like to acknowledge the following people for their contributions, without which this book could never have been created:

Anne Walradt for her sacrifice, hard work, and countless hours editing stories. Besides her love for romance writing and her expertise, as president of the New Jersey Romance Writers she recruited and influenced several outstanding authors to contribute quality stories. It was fate and a blessing that I found Anne and she agreed to be part of the team.

Tymm Smith for his hard work and expertise in designing the cover and book. I appreciate him going above and beyond the call of duty to ensure the success of *Romance Recipes for the Soul*.

Carol Stacy and all of the following, who found it in their hearts to give such wonderful testimonials: Connie Messina, Anna LoBello, Joe Ferro, Susan Arnold, Marlene Wegner, Mike Meunier, Denice Janik, Karen Kennedy, Jack Shrum, Ginny Hart, Ricky Baker, Connie Forzano, Kristin Kelly, and Lyn Wagner.

New Jersey Romance Writers and all the contributing authors.

Contents

Author's Note 10

Reading Our Recipes 11

Ingredients & Substitutions 13

Techniques 16

❤

1. Recipes that Cost less than $40

❤

Chinese Food on the Beach   *Frank Cabiroy* 19

A Dash of Celestial Seasoning   *Sandy Ferguson* 23

Snowed   *Anne Frazier* 28

Poetry in Motion   *Holly Love* 34

Crème d'amour   *Ruth MacLean* 39

Duck Soup   *Patsy Moore* 43

Seeing Things Differently   *Sean Toner* 49

Birthday à la King   *Lorraine Coyle* 53

Tailgate Mystery Date   *Gail Woods Thompson* 57

Aunt Rita's Sugar Cookies   *Elizabeth Keys* 61

One Hot Fajita   *Robert S. Cohen* 65

Contents

2. RECIPES THAT COST LESS THAN $80

Stormy Weather in the Living Room
Michael Matteo   71

Soft Center Special   *Sue Emms*   75

Power Play   *Kathryn Quick*   79

Late Christmas Dinner Surprise   *Mario I. Oña*   83

New Year's Eve, Alone Together   *Patricia Leary*   88

One Less Angel   *Robert S. Cohen*   94

Surprise Scavenger Hunt   *Chelle Martin*   98

Bicycle Built for Two   *Patricia Leary*   103

Champagne Kisses   *Colleen H. Admirand*   109

Lost in Love   *Leslie Rogalski*   114

One Small Step   *Robert S. Cohen*   118

Wish on the Moon   *Lyn Palmer*   122

Catch of the Day   *Sue Emms*   126

3. RECIPES THAT COST LESS THAN $120

Me, a Little Girl, and a Big Fish
Frank Cabiroy / Nancy Quatrano   133

Take Me Out to the Ball Game   *Mary Stella*   137

Cruise to a Deserted Island   *Penelope A. Marzec*   142

Relationship Repair   *Carole Duncan Buckman*   145

Contents

The Fall(-ing in Love) Guy   *Sue Emms*   151

The Rose   *James Mitchell*   155

Half a Ring   *Lynn Whited Hutton*   161

A Knight to Remember   *Michael Matteo*   166

4. RECIPES THAT COST LESS THAN $160

Scrumptious Saturday   *Nancy Quatrano*   173

Ham and Rye on a Harley   *Sharon L. Konschak*   177

The Business of Love   *Sue Emms*   182

Cinderella   *Jim Novotny*   186

Kidnapped   *Lynn Whited Hutton*   193

5. RECIPES THAT COST MORE THAN $160

Helicopters & Horses   *Sue Emms*   199

East Meets West: A Double Date Surprise *Jon Queijo*   203

Typical Dinner and a Movie? NOT!

   Frank Cabiroy / Nancy Quatrano   209

ABOUT THE AUTHOR   218

ABOUT THE EDITOR   218

CONTRIBUTORS   219

READER'S REVIEW   223

SUBMIT A STORY   224

Author's Note

DATING STRENGTHENS relationships, enriches lives, creates positive memories, and gives you something to look forward to. Everyone needs to date to feel special, to feel excited, and to keep that spark alive.

Romance Recipes for the Soul is a collection of personal dating stories that are imaginative, thoughtful, and unique. These aren't your typical "let's go to dinner and movies" dates.

The dates are formatted like recipes you would find in a cookbook. The "recipes" list ingredients, cost, preparation time, and more. In addition, these "recipes" will stimulate creative techniques and offer possible ingredient substitutions.

The collection of favorite recipes will simplify planning a special date and guarantee delicious results. And the best part—it's not fattening!

In time, the romance flame cools down. As we get more comfortable with the one we love, romance often takes a back seat to lesser things. It doesn't have to be this way. In the course of every great romance, there's at least one great meal. From Chinese food on the beach served under moonlight and stars to medieval victuals devoured in the midst of knights and dragons, these stories are guaranteed to get you and your sweetheart in the mood for love.

Whether you're looking for love, working to build a lasting relationship, or trying to put a bit of romance back into your present relationship, this book will help.

—FRANK CABIROY

Reading Our Recipes

The recipes throughout this book are simple to read and follow, thanks to these standard features:

 Preparation
Time
Each Recipe provides an at-a-glance time for preparation.

Fast	**Under one hour**
Moderate	**One to two hours**
Long	**More than two hours**

 Chef

The recommended gender to prepare the meal.

Male or Female

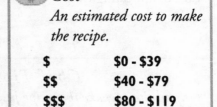 Cost
An estimated cost to make the recipe.

$	**$0 - $39**
$$	**$40 - $79**
$$$	**$80 - $119**
$$$$	**$120 - $159**
$$$$$	**$160 +**

Ingredients
A checklist of items needed for the recipe.

>   Chinese food (take-out)
>
>   Blanket
>
>   Bottle of sparkling wine
>
>   Picnic basket
>
>   Wine glasses

Recipe
Directions to prepare and serve the meal.

I SPENT SEVERAL of my teenage years on the sunny California sand playing beach boy. Never planned to leave the Golden State. Then my firm relocated me to Virginia Beach. The sun didn't seem quite as bright there until I met Ann, one of my new coworkers. She had the full package—a rare combination of appealing traits.

❤ Chef Tips ❤
Helpful tips to make the recipe just right.

1. Use real wine glasses and pack them carefully.

2. Make sure that your beach blanket is clean.

Ingredients & Substitutions

*T*HE RECIPES are suggestions promoting romance and telling how to sustain romance in a relationship. They provide a list of ingredients and serving tips for each romantic recipe.

Modifications and substitutions are encouraged to satisfy your specific taste. Sustaining romance in relationships can take some creativity and imagination, so please use them when substituting. *Romance Recipes for the Soul* provides tested recipes for seasoning and savoring romance, which will sweeten your love life.

Just like any ordinary recipe, any ingredient can be substituted according to the chef's taste. For instance, if the recipe calls for a bottle of wine and you don't drink alcohol, substitute sparkling cider. On the other hand, if the recipe calls for a beach setting and you live in the Midwest, improvise and go to a park or your favorite place. This can be done for any recipe listed in this book. The following ingredients can be used for substitutions. The best substitutions will come from the chef. The following will stimulate your creative and imaginative juices. Let them flow!

❤ Write a Love poem for your Sweetheart.
❤ Take a Horse-drawn Carriage ride.
❤ Swim in the Moonlight.
❤ Walk through the Woods.

💜 Take an evening boat ride.

💜 Picnic in front of the fireplace.

💜 Wander through a botanical garden.

💜 Visit a museum.

💜 See a laser show at a planetarium.

💜 Go for a Foliage drive.

💜 Dine in candlelight.

💜 Watch a stage show.

💜 Massage your partner's feet.

💜 Slip a love note under the pillow.

💜 Create a collage using photographs of Each other.

💜 Send a love telegram expressing your feelings.

💜 Send pink roses; they carry the message, "You're gentle and Graceful."

💜 Send light pink roses; they convey "admiration."

💜 Send red roses; they symbolize "love, respect, and courage."

💜 Send deep pink roses; they say, "Thank you."

💜 Send a single white rose; it says, "You're Heavenly."

💜 Send red and white roses tied together; they indicate "unity."

💜 Send yellow roses; they signify "Joy and gladness."

💜 Send a Bouquet of roses in full bloom; it means "gratitude."

💜 Send a single Rose in full bloom; it means "I love you" or "I still love you."

💜 Insert a love note in his pocket or her purse.

💜 Frame your favorite love letter and hang it on the wall.

💜 Drop by your sweetheart's place of work with a little Gift.

💜 Frame your baby pictures together.

💜 Place an ad in the newspaper expressing your Love.

💜 Send a balloon bouquet.

💜 Hide a box of Chocolates under the pillow.

♥ Hide a manicure gift certificate for her to find.

♥ Mail a greeting card.

♥ Place a flower arrangement in the refrigerator.

♥ Leave a Romantic message on the answering machine.

♥ E-mail a Romantic message.

♥ Fax a Romantic message.

♥ Write a message with lipstick on the bathroom mirror.

♥ Place a note to meet you for dinner under the windshield wiper.

♥ Give a sexy wake-up call.

♥ Mail a love letter.

♥ Call your Sweetheart just to say, "Hello."

♥ Play Hooky together from work.

♥ Get home earlier than your mate and have dinner ready.

♥ Send a box of Chocolates to the office.

♥ Write a letter stating all the reasons that he/she is special to you.

♥ Mail an X-rated letter.

♥ Send booklet of Love coupons.

♥ Picnic in the den.

♥ Horseback ride through the woods.

♥ Go for a walk in the rain.

♥ Hide some lingerie in his brief case.

♥ Meet in public wearing a disguise.

♥ Show up wearing just your Teddy under your coat.

♥ Give a full body bath scrub.

♥ Feed him/her Blindfolded.

♥ Hide a gift to be discovered in the course of a daily routine.

♥ Give a surprise gift at a restaurant. Make arrangements with the server in advance.

Techniques

WHAT MAKES a successful date? Besides being with the one you care about, the elements are fairly simple. It's not always what you specifically do on a date that will make it special and capture the other's heart; it's the thoughtfulness that goes into it. With love being the driving force, other components such as creativity and imagination will come naturally.

The most creative ideas come from beginners, not experts. Love is in the details. Romance is synonymous with love, and love comes from the heart. Therefore, throw your heart into it, and the rest will follow.

The recipes in this book have proven to be a delicious success for the people involved. They are tried and true recipes that come from real people like you. Although the recipes are there for you to follow, they may need that special ingredient only you can provide. Bon Appétit.

I.

RECIPES
THAT COST
LESS THAN
$40

Love is patient and kind. Love is not jealous, it does not brag, and it is not proud. Love is not rude, is not selfish and does not get upset with others. Love does not count up wrongs that have been done. Love is not happy with evil but is happy with the truth. Love patiently accepts all things. It always trusts, always hopes, and always remains strong.

1 COR. 13: 4–7

Chinese Food on the Beach

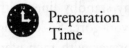

Preparation Time

Fast

Cost

$

Chef

Male or Female

This date is sure to win anyone over—showing the creative, romantic person you really are.

Ingredients

Chinese food (take-out)

Blanket

Bottle of sparkling wine

Picnic basket

Wine glasses

I SPENT SEVERAL of my teenage years on the sunny California sand playing beach boy. Never planned to leave the Golden State. Then my firm relocated me to Virginia Beach. The sun didn't seem quite as bright there until I met Ann, one of my new coworkers. She had the full package—a rare combination of appealing traits. She had a great sense of humor, a winning personality, a great job, and an incredible beauty that would stop any man in his footsteps just for a glimpse.

Ann was different from the overblown California beauties I had dated. Her beauty was enhanced by her innocence and small-town values—the kind of values that bring men to their knees at the altar.

As I settled in, I tried some of my standby lines with Ann. She looked at me with her you-gotta-be-kidding look. I figured she'd been hassled forever with men who saw only her prettiness. I decided I'd been stupid to waste her time with lines. If I liked her all that much, I ought to invest in some genuine attention. I started spending more time with her in meetings, conferences, and private discussions. Her positive attitude and sense of the ridiculous kept the whole group laughing. We discovered we both liked in-line skating, professional football, ocean waves at night, and Chinese food—the hotter the better (even though I break out in a sweat). The more I saw of her, the more I liked her. When she continued to turn aside my suggestions for dinner and the movies, I decided I'd have to do something special. I had to get her attention. I checked out all the Chinese restaurants and finally found one even better than the best I'd found in California.

I checked the calendar for a big moon and an incoming tide. Then I invited her out for a Chinese dinner at a moonlit beach. She went for it.

Friday night I called the Chinese restaurant and ordered an array of Ann's favorite dishes. I packed the trunk with all the essentials for the perfect date with the perfect girl. I put in the beach blanket—to sit on later, but now to cushion the old wicker picnic basket my mom courted my dad with. It held the best bottle of sparkling wine I could find and two tall crystal wineglasses. I took my turbo-charged

Nissan 300ZX to the car wash on the way to pick up the Chinese food, which I also hid in the basket, smothering it all in the beach quilt to keep it hot—and so she wouldn't smell it.

When I picked Ann up, laughter danced across her face when she saw my car, making her more beautiful than I had ever seen her. "So," she said, once she settled in, "where's this fabulous Chinese restaurant? I don't know of any nearby."

"Restaurant?" I replied. "I didn't say 'restaurant.' I promised fabulous Chinese food. And that's what I'm going to deliver." I grinned, feeling like the wolf in "Little Red Riding Hood."

Once we arrived near the oceanfront, I pulled down a side street by a secluded area of the beach. I turned off the car, handed her out of it with a soft kiss to her palm, then headed for the trunk to get my supplies. "Shall we?" I said, taking her hand again in one of mine and carrying the basket and blanket in the other.

We headed toward the sand and picked out a smooth spot, slightly raised so we could see the waves breaking. I stretched out the blanket, poured the wine, and began to set out the food—Orange Beef, Hunan Jumbo Shrimp, Broccoli with Garlic Sauce (if we both ate it, we'd be fine!). I served Ann, just as a gentleman would. I turned so I could see her face silhouetted by streaks of orange and purple shooting across the sky behind her. We were just finishing up when the sun settled and sank. The timing was perfect. As Ann sipped on the wine, looking out into the water, I caught her smiling. More than smiling really—she was beaming. "This is very special," she said quietly. I got the feeling that no one had made her feel special in a long time.

After dinner, we talked, we laughed, and sometimes we just listened to the sound of the waves crashing in. When a cool breeze came through, I slipped a sweater over her sun-kissed shoulders and then nestled her in my arms.

Before long, we were kissing under the stars. "There's a full moon tonight," I whispered.

"Yes," she replied. "It's the brightest night I've ever seen."

FRANK CABIROY

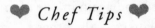

❤ *Chef Tips* ❤

1. Use real wine glasses and pack them carefully.

2. Make sure that your beach blanket is clean.

3. Check the weather conditions before you make the date.

A Dash of Celestial Seasoning

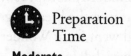

Preparation Time
Moderate

Cost
$

Chef
Male or Female

*This date is for anyone who wants to let a
"special someone" know that he lights up her
life (or she lights up his).*

Ingredients

Bottle of wine

Appetizers

Relaxing music

Toy truck

Babysitter

Blanket

Blindfold / bandanna

Glow-in-the-dark stars and moons sticker set

*J*ASON AND I have been married for twelve years.
With two children and a business to run, our hectic schedules leave little time for us to share quiet
moments. One winter evening as I raced home from a
dreaded food shopping run, I realized I had to make time
to be alone with my husband. I had to let him know how

much he truly meant to me and how much I appreciated him. As I pulled into our driveway, I glanced up at the sky. I slammed on the brakes when one of our most memorable nights came crashing into my mind. My abrupt foot action also sent the laundry detergent into the bread bag, but this time I didn't care if the bread went from Wonder to wounded. I had to prepare for a special date.

On the night Jason had professed his love for me, the moon hung three-quarters full in a sky radiant with an abundance of glittering white stars. We'd driven to the mountains in his old pickup truck. Jason pulled the tailgate down so we could sit outside, drink our wine, and enjoy the view. After Jason said he loved me, he asked me to look up at the sky. He pointed and, in a serious tone, vowed that he would always strive to make me happy. "I promise to give you the stars," he murmured. The passion and urgency in his kiss that night warms me still.

I believed those words and gave my heart to him that evening. But how could I recreate that night with two feet of hard-packed snow covering the ground? I love the guy, but I'm not into having my buns freeze to the tailgate of his truck while we sip on ice-pops. No. This date had to be as warm and romantic as that summer evening in the mountains.

I thought about ideas all night, but it wasn't until the next morning that I figured out a way to duplicate one of our most unforgettable times together. I called my mom and arranged for her to take the children. I then called Jason and told him that I had a surprise for him, but that he had to be home at seven that evening, no sooner, no later. Of course he was puzzled, but he agreed. By six forty-five, I had changed and set up a tray with cheese, crackers, and a bottle of wine in the family room. I didn't put out goblets because back in the days of hanging out in his truck, we swigged the wine right from the bottle. I popped in one of my relaxation tapes featuring sounds heard only in the forest. I laughed as I put the tape on, for I had never listened to it. I never have time just to relax and listen to music. With two young kids, I often listen to children's songs, and the repetition of the lyrics serves to calm only my children. The chipmunk-sounding voices do little to soothe me. In fact, they often grate on my nerves until I feel like I'm being skinned by a cartoon character wielding a potato peeler.

I looked at the clock. I had five minutes and one important thing left to do. I ran to the garage, then dragged my toddler's battery-operated kid-sized pickup truck into the house. I set it near the blanket I had placed on the floor and let the tailgate down.

Jason walked in the door just as the chime rang seven o'clock. "What's this?" he asked, obviously confused by my hiking outfit.

I pulled out a bandanna from the back pocket of my shorts and held it up to him. "It's all part of my surprise," I whispered.

Jason grinned as I blindfolded him. "Do we get to play blind man's bluff in the buff?"

I gave him a playful punch, then led him down the hall and into the family room. I shut off the light, then helped him walk to the center of the room. Gently, I eased him down to sit on the blanket. "Okay," I said, kneeling beside him, "you can take off the bandanna."

He clutched my hand as he gazed up to the ceiling. The sparkly glow-in-the-dark stickers I had applied that afternoon provided us with a celestial blend of stars and moons. The light spangled the room and danced across his dear face.

"This is great," he replied in his deep, sexy voice.

I snuggled against his chest. "Does it remind you of anything?" I asked.

"Honey, how could I ever forget the first time I told you I loved you? It was the best night of my life."

He kissed me and my heart soared. A few moments later, he pulled away. He slapped his hand against the open tailgate of our son's truck. "I miss that old hunk of metal. Do you think we'll fit on the back of this one?" he teased.

I started to laugh, but he cut me off with another passionate kiss. "I vow to make you happy for the rest of your life," he whispered.

"That's what this is for," I breathed in reply. "I wanted to show you how much I appreciate you. You made me happy then; you make me happy now. You have given me the stars, honey."

He hugged me. "Speaking of stars, where did our two cute comets go tonight?"

I smiled. "They're streaking across my mom's living room at this very moment."

While we drank from the bottle of wine, we reminisced about the crazy, spontaneous things we did before we had the kids—like the time we took our rent money and used it to scalp tickets to a rock concert, and the days we would just lie in bed to watch old Tarzan movies. Our conversation soon turned to the times we've shared since having the children. We laughed. Gone were the days of staying in bed past 7 A.M. or even thinking of using the mortgage money to buy concert tickets. But we both agreed that while the night we had recreated had been a special moment, being together in our own "family" room gave our date an even deeper meaning.

The artificial stars eventually began to dim, but as we lay there, locked in an embrace, I knew my heart would always belong to this man. Like the real stars, our love will shine forever bright.

SANDY FERGUSON

♥ *Chef Tips* ♥

1. The glow-in-the-dark stickers need to be "preheated" by a light bulb. The longer you "cook" your stars and moons, the better; this enhances their brightness and their longevity.

2. If you can have this date outside, a real pickup truck will suffice.

Snowed

 Preparation Time

 Cost

 Chef

Fast

$

Male

Even a simple date can lead to your heart's desire.

Ingredients

Snow

Hill with a long view

Toboggan

Warm clothing

Hot chocolate in a thermos

I SPENT MY GIRLHOOD in the desert. I love the long vistas, the red rocks, the high mesas, and the distant rim of purple mountains. I love the cacti, the unexpected wildflowers, the secret water sources. But most, I love the heat, the bright sun, the high blue daytime sky obscuring nighttime stars beyond imagining.

But when real life seized control, I found myself trapped in the north, in the winter, working at a ski lodge surrounded by snowbunnies and ski fanatics, and cold, cold, cold. Everything was blizzard white, and I couldn't see beyond those dratted trees. Don't think I didn't give the place a chance. I did. I tried ice skating, but my fragile ankles dropped me to the ice where I curled up and skidded around like a hockey puck. I went skiing and broke Guinness records for times back on my feet and filling in sitzmarks. I needed a fur factory to stay warm, but I don't think there are any in Idaho.

So I talked the boss out of the ski rental booth cashier job and into the kitchen-serf-at-the-stove job. It wasn't much fun, but at least I was warm while I plotted my return to Coyote Country.

Then the boss hired a new guy. This one wasn't a slick ski instructor who laughed when I went down. John was tall and lanky, with a lazy grin, a slow wink, a mustache, and he knew horses. He ran the winter camping trips into the backcountry.

I stayed away from him because I have a serious weakness for the tall lanky ones who know how to work hard and play hard. But I don't like hairy upper lips. So when he came sneaking into the kitchen for some hot chocolate after getting back from a trip one day, I figured I was safe enough for a short exposure even if I was nigh onto crazy with cabin fever.

I was wrong.

He grinned and winked at me, and I might as well have given up my heart right then. But I'm a fighter.

So when he said, "I've got the rest of the afternoon off. Want to go for a ride?" I laughed.

"You're joking, right? What's the wind chill today? Minus 23°? Nothing would make me leave this nice warm kitchen."

"Nothing?" He looked at me, head cocked to one side.

"Nothing. And I'm certainly not getting on one of those monsters you call horses." I should've known from experience not to give a salesman anything to latch onto and argue against.

"I wasn't planning to take the horses," he said mildly. "I thought I'd get out one of the toboggans and try South Slope."

Well, I thought, *toboggans may toss you off, but they don't bite.*

"I've been feeling a mite closed in," he said. "Spent the last five days in the deep forest camp. I need the long view again. It's clear today; oughta be able to see sixty miles from the top."

I wavered. "Where's South Slope? I haven't found anywhere with a view past the trees."

"You haven't been skiing?"

I didn't say anything. No point in going into how short the view is from a sitzmark on the baby hill.

"It's kind of hot in here, don't you think?" he asked, running his finger around his collar.

I'd noticed it'd gotten a bit warmer since he'd come in, but I didn't see any reason to mention that. "I like it."

"Mmmmm. Tell you what. I'll bring an extra goose-down coat. You bring the hot chocolate. I'll guarantee you the best view you'll ever see." He looked at me, challenge in his eyes.

"Maybe," was the best I could do. But I'd about decided the far view might be worth the cold, just this once.

"See you in a hour," he said as he put his cowboy hat on and left.

I thought it odd that the kitchen got smaller after he left. Closed in on me. Maybe it was the scent of pine he took with him when he closed the door.

I took a big thermos of hot chocolate and met him by the toboggans. He hit me with that lazy grin again and stuffed me into the promised coat. I felt pretty warm for the moment.

He hauled that sled onto the ski lift with us and we rode up the mountain, over the treetops. I could see again. I could breathe, too. The air was dry, like the desert air I was used to.

We got out at the top of the ski run. I looked down that slide into oblivion and balked. "Hey," he called, "you coming?" He was twenty feet away, dragging that toboggan, and headed for the other side of the peak. "You're gonna get real cold real fast if you just stand there." I picked up my nearly rooted feet and scrambled after him.

He reached for my mittened hand just as we got to the peak. "What do you think?" He turned south. I looked.

He'd been right. Sixty miles easily. Foothills at our feet. Valleys and plains beyond. And in the farthest reaches, purple mountains.

We took the toboggan down a winding slope that curved back and forth around and down the mountain. I rode snuggled in his arms, the icy air whistling past my face and making my eyes tear, and our laughter ringing through the trees.

At the bottom of the mountain, he grinned and said, "Well? Want to go back to your cozy warm kitchen or make another run?"

I threw caution to the winds and grinned back. "Another run, please." We took the ski lift up again. We crashed on the second run down, rolling over and over in the snow, clutching each other like playing polar bears. With all my practice getting into the record books, I was first on my feet and gave him a hand to help him stand. I got a good look into his eyes. I hadn't noticed their color back in the kitchen when he'd winked at me. Trying too hard not to notice, I expect. Now I saw their color. Brown. Warm brown.

Since the cold wasn't bothering me much, we took another run. I could get used to the view, followed by the speed, the excitement, the safe arrival. We took the last ride up the lift and arrived at the top just in time to see the sunset spread its reds and pinks and purples across the valleys and on to the mountains. It looked a bit like home. John found a space sheltered from the wind in front of a copse of trees, and we settled down on the toboggan to drink our hot chocolate and wait for moonrise and light enough for our last ride.

"Why hasn't anyone else been on our toboggan run?" I asked him.

"No one knows about it," he said. "I found it the day after I got here. It needed a little clearing before I lured you out."

"You planned this?" I looked into those warm brown eyes again. "For me?"

He ducked his head. Then lifted it and stared at the rising moon and those stars floating in infinity. "Yeah."

"Why?"

"You look like a woman who seeks heat."

It's true. I am. So I reached for him, mustache and all, and found it.

ANNE FRAZIER

♥ *Chef Tips* ♥

1. It's better to stash the thermos of hot chocolate somewhere than to carry it with you on the toboggan.
2. Take a blanket and stash it, too.
3. If you can find a hill and get up it without lift tickets, the cost drops to almost nothing.
4. A toboggan may be replaced with a sled, flying saucer, or large piece of cardboard.

Poetry in Motion

 Preparation
Time

Fast

 Cost

$

Chef

Male or Female

*An evening of poetic expression sure to set the
perfect stage for romance.*

Ingredients

Local event schedules

Paper and pens

Bookstore

Drinks and dessert

A S SOON AS I met Ben in a poetry
writing class, I knew I wanted to get to
know him better. Whenever I read my
poems aloud, I could feel his eyes riveted on my face. And
I was wildly impressed with his beautiful poems about
relationships. When I asked him for a copy of one of his
sonnets, his eyes lit up. That's when I began cooking up a
plan for our first date.

Ben was obviously shy though, so I knew it would be
up to me to suggest that we get together outside of class.
To appear casual, I simply asked him if he had ever been

to the monthly poetry readings at the local bookstore. When he said no, I told him the date and time of the next reading and mentioned that I'd be going. When he wrote the event on his pocket calendar and said, "I'll be there," my heart hit Indy 500 speed.

I arrived early to the event and saved us two seats in a cozy corner. When Ben showed up, he gave me a bigger smile than I'd ever seen on his face.

Other poets began sharing their work. Between readings, Ben and I whispered our commentary to each other on the subjects and styles, and, as I expected, his observations were particularly insightful. After about half an hour, I asked him if he'd brought any of his poems to read aloud.

"No, I figured I'd just listen," he said with a shrug.

"Well, I brought something," I replied. Then I showed him my copy of his poem from class, "The Writer's Heart." He looked embarrassingly flattered.

"Really? You want to read that?" he finally said.

"I would be honored."

He nodded his approval, and I read his poem to the group. I made a point of looking up at him right after reading the line, "Two lovers floating like words in the dark."

After I returned to my seat, Ben pointed to my writing folder and asked me, "You must have a poem of your own with you . . . how about 'Face of a Dreamer'?"

My heart instantly beat faster. I'd read that poem on the first day of class two months before, and he'd remembered the title. I was thrilled that I happened to have it with me. Soon Ben stood at the podium reading my poem.

After the readings, we explored the poetry section of the bookstore. Standing on opposite sides of a low shelving unit, we read titles of poems to each other and tried to guess the poets.

"Love's Humility," he said.

"Emily Dickinson," I said and flashed him an impish grin. "Ok, I bet there's no way you'll ever get this one: 'Shall I Compare Thee to a Summer's Day?'"

He teased me back. "Oh, wait, it's on the tip of my tongue. Some English guy from the Sixteenth Century. 'Bill' somebody."

"The Immortal Shakespeare." I used a teenager's awestruck voice.

"Never heard of him. Is his poetry as good as yours?"

I laughed, clasped my hands to my chest, and said with an exaggeratedly wistful tone, "And to think just a few months ago, I'd never heard of you."

I was glad Ben came up with a reason for the evening to continue. "You know what's even better for the soul than poetry?"

"Oh, I don't know . . . self-actualization? Reaching higher consciousness? Forsaking judgment?"

"Uh-huh," he said, "and also dessert." Soon we were sitting at a table drinking French sodas and splitting a chocolate chip muffin.

"So tell me," I asked, "what do you like best about writing poetry?"

"Well, maybe it's that the poem is completely mine. On the other hand, it's kind of a lonely activity," he answered, touching my hand and stressing the word "lonely."

I thought for a minute. "Doesn't have to be, you know. Have you ever collaborated on a poem with someone else?"

"No, actually, I can't say that I have."

"Well," I continued, pulling out lined paper and two pens, "here's an interesting way I know of to write a keeper of a poem. You write the first line. Then you pass me the paper, and I'll write the second line, and so on. We pass the paper back and forth until someone has the guts to write the ending. Voilà! Instant joint poetry."

"Let's get to it!" Ben responded.

It was easier than I could have imagined for each of us to write the next line in perfect harmony with the previous one:

Love is the impassioned wave
That greets the beveled shore,
Fluid, constant, stalwart blue,
Mothered by young Earth's core,
Reaching from the captive's heart
Through its paths protected,
Tainted not by mortal force,
Nor by doubt affected.
Shunning time's obtrusive hands,
Embracing every storm,
Using each obstacle's might
To brace its earnest form.
Here, only human, we stand
Bathed by the rhythmic spray,
Souls imbued with the luster
Of ardent tides in sway.
Love is this endless current
Forever in our midst,
Granting our spirits rapture
If we embrace its gifts.

As he walked me to my car, Ben said, "You know, I'm going to want my own copy of the poem we wrote. How about you make one and give it to me when we have dinner together Saturday night?"

I grinned at his creative way of asking to see me again. "That sounds like a great idea," I said.

"Have you ever been to *Chez* Wheeler?"

I batted my eyelashes. "Wheeler" was his last name. "No, I don't believe I have."

"It's at 1331 Essex Avenue. I'll be sure to make reservations at seven o'clock for their best table."

"Wonderful," I said. "Can I bring anything?"

"Yes," Ben replied, touching my shoulder. "The chef is guaranteed to make you something extra special if you read original poetry aloud to him while he's cooking."

I felt a warm tingle throughout my body. "I'll be sure to bring my entire repertoire," I told him. I gave him my most demure smile and then drove away. It looked like our second date would be even more romantic than the first.

HOLLY LOVE

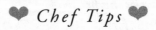

♥ *Chef Tips* ♥

1. Poetry readings can easily be found at national bookstore chains.

2. Study up on poetry titles for the guessing game!

3. Use brand new felt tip pens—one blue and one red—to write the joint poem.

Crème d'amour

 Preparation Time

Moderate

 Cost

$

 Chef

Male or Female

This recipe, like many good ones, has enjoyed the test of time. It is the type of recipe that can be made any hour of the day or night and can be used in any situation requiring tenderness and understanding.

Ingredients

Bathtub filled with scented bath water

Music ("Moonlight Sonata")

Soft light and firelight

Bottle of red wine (Merlot)

Brie cheese and melba rounds

IM CLOSED THE DOOR and smiled at me. "Glad to be home?"

"You know I am." I bit back a yawn. "Airless rooms. Endless meetings. And you?"

"Endless stew."

I grinned. "Poor baby. Home alone with only my stew to keep you warm."

He rolled a strand of my hair around his fingers. "Did you know your stew and the Energizer bunny have something in common?"

I laughed. "They both just keep on—"

"You got it," he said as he peeled my coat off my shoulders and threw it over the back of a chair. "And you've had enough for one day," he said as his fingers traced small circles along my shoulders. "Why don't you go upstairs?"

The musical notes his fingers played, as they moved up along my tense neck muscles, helped me relax. "What would I do without you?" I touched his cheek, and his lips followed my fingers.

"You're never going to get the chance to find out." He turned me around to face the stairs and whispered in my ear, "Up you go."

I went upstairs to our bed, stretched out on its satiny smoothness and fell asleep. I awakened to the rumble of the water cascading into the tub and recognized the beginning steps of a special ritual. I tiptoed to the bathroom. My husband was waiting, his anxious glance revealing his concern for me. Twenty years of marriage told me Jim was doing the one thing he knew would ease the exhaustion clinging to my shoulders like a cloak. "Just for me?" I asked, my heart pounding with pleasure as I watched him add bath gel to the water.

The corners of his lips lifted in a half smile. "No, silly, I do this for all the women in my life."

My spirits rose. "I'll just bet you do. Even the cat."

He pointed at the bubble-laden water. "Strip and hop in, or I'll be forced to take appropriate action."

Daring him to make a move, I loosened the knot on my bathrobe. "Or you'll issue a summons, counselor?"

He wrapped his arms around me. "Don't tempt a man on a mission. I'm here to save the woman I love."

"Thank God," I said and sank into his embrace.

As the gardenia-scented water of the bath enclosed me, I shut my eyes and let my thoughts drift away from the moment toward the distinctive sounds emanating from the bedroom—sounds that told me Jim was getting out my favorite negligee and turning down the bed. The muffled pop of a cork heralded the opening of a bottle of Merlot. The clink and soft whooshing sound announced the lighting of the propane fireplace at the foot of the bed. In my mind's eye, the flickering golden tones of light cast the room in a bronze glow. As if on cue, the haunting strains of "Moonlight Sonata" drifted toward me.

Peering around the door, he held my burgundy bathrobe out in front of him, matador style. "Madame, your evening awaits you."

"This is your summons, I assume?" I gave him my best chin-tucked lawyer's glance and slid down to shoulder depth.

He pulled a thick white towel from the warming rack and twirled it over his head as he approached the tub. "I assure you it's the most important invitation you've had in a while."

"And when was the last invitation of this sort?" I ran my toes along the upper edge of the tub and watched as he sat down on the edge, the towel in his hands.

"A gentleman never tells." He gave me his patented wolf-in-sheep's-clothing look. "Are you coming out or am I getting in?"

Enjoying the banter, I snuggled farther into the water. "I'll get back to you on that."

He grabbed my hand and pulled. "No. You won't."

I stepped from the tub and slipped the towel around

me. "Would you like to change your client's plea, counselor?" I asked.

He slipped the robe around me and pulled me into the warm circle of his arms. "Not on your life. We have a deal, remember? We're repeat offenders."

Pretending not to know what he was talking about, I asked, "We are?"

"Yes. We've been doing this for years." He scooped me into his arms. The cloak of exhaustion had been exchanged for a robe of expectation. My husband was giving me the date of my dreams. He was recreating the most important date we had ever shared: our wedding night.

RUTH MACLEAN

♥ *Chef Tips* ♥

1. A date can be as important to a marriage as it is to a courtship. A date between two married people can reaffirm their need for connection and their need to shut the world out of the relationship, so they can rekindle the love and sense of togetherness they shared when they married.

2. Candles can be used in place of a fireplace or added for extra atmosphere.

Duck Soup

L Preparation
Time

Fast

$ Cost

$

Chef

Male or Female

*This date is either for the woman or man who
wants a date to share the enjoyment of the outdoor
sport of duck hunting.*

Ingredients

*Any canned soups, stews, or homemade duck soup,
if available*

Special crackers and cheese

Flavored coffee

Several large thermos bottles for food and coffee

Tablecloth with matching napkins

*Cold weather hunting clothes (or proper clothes
for other sports)*

M Y BOYFRIEND was an avid duck
hunter, and I was unfamiliar with
that part of his life. As the opening
day of the season approached, I told him I wanted to go
with him to experience what he talked about so reverently.
I was touched when he received my request so enthusias-

tically and dragged me off to the sporting goods store where he outfitted me for the trip.

"Why do I need these funny looking clothes?"

"If you're not in camouflage, the ducks can spot you and won't come close enough."

"Oh, I see," I said, but I didn't. "Does this jump suit have to be so padded?"

I negotiated my way to a chair and attempted in vain to hook my rubber boots. He tried not to laugh.

"Now, I know what the Pillsbury dough boy feels like," I said.

"You'll need these special clothes. It's cold. The winds are brisk, and if it rains you can get wet in the duck blind."

"Oh, I see." I was beginning to see I might have made a mistake. However, I was determined. There had to be more to this than sitting out in the cold wet wind, using a call to quack like a demented duck, and shooting a few itsy-bitsy birds. Either that, or this guy was nuts and not all I thought he was. One way or the other I had to find out.

The day of the hunt arrived. He picked me up at the ridiculous hour of 3:30—yes, that's A.M. During a quick breakfast at a local café, he bobbed like a jack-in-the-box with excitement. But 4:45 found us gliding silently over the pitch black lake. Something large splashed close to the boat. Ducks? Nutria? Snakes? Alligators? *Big* alligators? Again, I considered that perhaps my judgment was a bit off.

With some radar-sharp sense of direction, he guided us through groups of cypress trees standing like people up to their knees in the cold lake water. After going under a railroad bridge, we found a channel through foot-tall water hyacinths. Finally, we reached our destination, the duck blind.

Again, I questioned my own sanity when he cautioned, "Just let me slip in first to make sure no snakes or other creatures have crawled up in here."

"Snakes! Poisonous ones?"

"It's too cold for them, but I don't want you worrying about anything like that no matter how remote the chance is."

After he checked the blind for critters—four, eight, or no-legged, I helped him unload the boat. Before long we had settled in on a rickety old wood bench. Though it was still dark, the inkiness had given way to a dark gray.

"Would you like me to show you how to use the duck call later?" he asked.

"Sure." I thought if I could play a child's kazoo I should be able to master a simple duck call.

I tried to remember all the things that he had told me about the various kinds of ducks—their calls, their flying and landing behaviors. He talked about how duck hunters sponsored proper management and conservation techniques so that ducks remained abundant and loss of habitat was being controlled. I listened and learned.

"Care to share and watch the sunrise?" he said. He gave me a cup of steaming black coffee and offered me his hand as he rose from the bench. Still holding my hand, he led me to a more open area of the blind where the roof disappeared and a waist-high exterior wall made possible a view of the expanse of the lake.

I was not prepared for the beauty that stretched before

me. Across the lake the sun rose over the horizon and shot rays of pink and orange through the stands of Spanish moss-draped cypress. A mist hovered over the lake, slowly rising off the water, where gently rocked at least a hundred ducks.

"John, look at all the ducks. Look at them."

When he laughed, I wondered why he wasn't worried about scaring them off. "They're decoys—you know, fake ducks."

"They look so real. When do we see the real thing?"

"Right now," he said, releasing my hand and putting down his own cup of coffee. He handed me my camera and told me to get some shots as he pointed to a large group of ducks flying out of the northeast. They circled back around again when he used the proper call, and the flock checked out the invitation from what they thought to be fellow ducks on the lake. They slowed their speed, descending to the lake. About a yard from the surface, the webbed feet extended, reaching for the water, and wings flared back as they glided for a landing.

The ducks came and went all morning. I got some great pictures. At noon I pulled out the thermos bottles full of piping hot soup and spread us a lunch of soup, crackers, cheese, fruit, and coffee. I appreciated his sharing this with me even if it was only a dry run for the opening day the following week when the shots would be with shotguns.

As the sun began to set and the scene before us was rivaled only by the one that morning, he asked, "Well, what did you think?"

"I can see why you love it, John. I'd like to come again."

"Even when we're shooting the ducks for real?" he asked.

"Yes, even then." I smiled.

He reached into the side pocket of his jump suit.

"I never thought I'd find a woman who understood my love of duck hunting. I felt I'd probably have to give it up if I married. I decided to bring this with me even though I feared you might hate hunting," he said, opening the blue velvet box in his hand. "It was beyond my greatest hopes to think that I might be able to share my life with someone who could understand and appreciate all this.

"I love you, Marie. Will you do me the honor of becoming my wife?" He moved the ring toward my hand.

"Are you telling me if I had hated this you would have still asked me to marry you?"

"Yes."

"And if I had hated it and asked you to give it up, you would have?"

"Yes."

"I love you, John." I blinked back tears as he slid the ring on my finger. "You'll never have to give up your duck hunting. Not now. Not ever."

PATSY MOORE

❤ *Chef Tips* ❤

1. This recipe is best served only to persons in long-term dating situations, rather than to first daters.

2. To make true duck soup: Take any good gumbo recipe and, instead of shrimp or sausage, use duck meat that has been boiled and deboned.

3. Serving the recipe: To make the meal special, even though it is being served in a duck blind and out of thermos bottles, take along a table-cloth and real napkins. The soups or stews make a nice meal when dressed up with special crackers, cheese, and fruit. Instead of regular coffee, choose a flavored one for fun.

4. Dressing inappropriately can ruin the date. Choose clothing well.

5. Can be applied to a variety of other outdoor sports and activities (fishing, deer hunting, camping, and hiking).

6. Clothing for the outing can be borrowed from someone else at no cost.

Seeing Things Differently

 Preparation Time

Fast

💰 Cost

$

👨‍🍳 Chef

Male or Female

A seemingly simple date with an unexpected twist.

Ingredients

Art museum

Silk scarf

AT FIRST, my date with Amanda seemed headed for disaster.

When I pulled up in front of her suburban Philadelphia, Tudor-style house, I found her waiting at the curb. Petite, dark-haired, and casually dressed in blue jeans and a tan sweater, Amanda looked better than most of the women I'd been set up with. She had a pretty face but kept her eyes hidden behind sunglasses, which I thought odd because the afternoon sky was overcast.

As I got out of the car, I wondered what she was hiding. I extended my hand and said, "It's nice to finally see you."

"I wish I could say the same," she answered, and ignored my hand. The word that came to my mind then, I cannot repeat now.

I opened the passenger door for her, and she climbed in awkwardly, her hand clutching at the seat. That made me think that perhaps she'd had too much to drink the night before and that her dark glasses were hiding bloodshot eyes.

Or worse, she was on drugs.

We talked as I drove toward the Brandywine Museum. I tried to make appropriate comments as she told me about her computer programming career, and she seemed genuinely interested as I related my attempts to sell novels.

After we got out of the car at the museum, she stood still by the car door instead of following me toward the entrance. I wanted to say, "Hey, what's your problem?" but politely asked, "Is something the matter?"

She stared into the distance, facing the highway instead of the Brandywine River or the rustic, barn-like museum. "I need to take your arm," she said.

So she was hung over, I thought. Too wobbly to even get into the museum on her own. "Would you like to go home?" I asked, unable to mask my annoyance.

She looked startled. "No, I . . ." Then comprehension lit her face. "Gina forgot to tell you that I'm blind?"

I was glad she couldn't see me turning red. "No," I forced from my throat. Then I couldn't help but ask, "Why did you want to come to an art museum?"

"Since I went blind four years ago, I've wanted to see art exhibits through someone else's eyes."

Amanda took my arm and I led her into the Brandywine. It didn't take me long to discover how differently I saw the world in the company of someone who saw none of it. I necessarily took notice of little things, like the width of doorways or the placement of people and common objects in a hallway or whether to step up or down, in order to guide Amanda's steps.

Things I'd taken for granted before—like the way rooms bathed in fluorescent light were brighter than rooms lit by sunny windows—caught my attention for the first time.

And then there were the paintings.

I led Amanda through gallery after gallery of three generations of Wyeth art work and through a wing dedicated to their contemporaries. She held my hand tightly and listened intently as I detailed the farm scenes, the Helga portraits, and the Maine paintings.

Standing before one of the Helgas, I described its setting—the tattered carpet under the subject's feet, the etched floorboards. Amanda turned to me and remarked in a low, confident voice, "I'll bet she's older." Amanda had seen, through my description of the painting's backdrop, Andrew Wyeth's intention to portray that his secret muse of so many years had aged.

Outside by the Brandywine River, we stood surprisingly close for two people who had met only a few hours earlier. In a soft voice, she asked, "Do you mind if I see what you look like?"

I already knew the answer, of course—I've seen movies—but to tease her, I asked, "How?"

"With my fingertips," she said, and then slowly traced my face with her fingers, running them along my nose and over my brows. She surveyed the line of my jaw and the curve of my chin as if gently painting fine details or sculpting an image of me in her mind. The day and her hand learning my face taught me how much I appreciate the privilege of sight and the power of touch.

I can't help thinking whether Chance or Fate or God brought me together with Amanda so that I would see the world in a brand new light.

SEAN TONER

❤ *Chef Tips* ❤

1. If your date isn't blind, blindfold him or her before going out together so that both of you can experience the world differently.

2. Location can be a museum, a park, a flower garden—whatever fits your desire.

Birthday à la King

 Preparation Time
Long

 Cost
$

Chef
Female

Uplifting and filling, even when time together is limited.

Ingredients

King Crab Salad

Imperial Hawaiian Meatballs and Rice

Cassette player

Royal music ("Hail to the Chief")

Jewel-encrusted Ice Cream (substitute colored sprinkles, if desired)

Blindfold

Royal Mints

One royal gown and crown

I WAS IN A FOUL MOOD. Actually I was royally ticked. Stuart, my significant other, had just dropped a water bomb on my parade. "I'm sorry," he apologized, "but the guy he lined up to cover for him called in sick. No one else but me is qualified to run those tests."

"But what about our date to celebrate your birthday? I had plans."

"He can't very well miss his own sister's wedding." Stuart ran his finger down my cheek. I closed my eyes to hide my disappointment. He kissed me. "Weddings are pretty important events," he said.

My eyes flickered open. Was this my Stuart saying this? The man who'd been shying from walking down the aisle for two years? Was he suddenly maturing as the count-down to his thirtieth birthday neared? "So, what's your schedule then?" I mumbled.

"I'll be home at 6:00 A.M., grab some sleep, and a quick bite, and get back to work by eight tomorrow evening, nine at the latest. The boss is giving me a bit of leeway. A birthday present."

"One whole hour to celebrate," I said sarcastically.

Stuart put his arms around me. "It's for a good cause, honey."

He kissed the soft spot on my neck, and I melted against him. "Bribery will get you nowhere. I'm holding you to our date even if you have only one eye open."

Stuart left to work his own Friday evening shift, and I paced the apartment, determined to make the best of it. I dug out a box from under the bed and flared my fingers over the lapels of the royal blue birthday dressing gown I'd bought for him. Wasn't it like Stuart to put himself out for a buddy? Just like he did for me. Instead of pout-ing, I should figure a way to show him how much I appreciated what a prince of a guy he truly was. My brain began to go clickety click. Could I still manage a date? Yes! I'd do it up in a grand way. I'd crown him, king for a day, maybe forever.

By four o'clock the next day, Stuart had been sleeping long enough, so I figured if I was going to pull off a proper coronation, it was time to wake him up. When I shook him awake, he peered up at me bleary-eyed, rolled himself more tightly into his blanket, hugged the pillow, and groaned.

"Come on, Stuart, you can't miss all of your birthday." I tugged at him.

Raising his head, he arched one dark brow at me. Tousled, he looked adorable and sexy. But right now, I had official business to attend to. He sniffed the air. "You cooked?" he asked.

"As though I don't do my share . . . ." I pummeled him with my fist, then rolled away from his grasp. "Dinner will be ready as soon as you shower."

By the time he came out of the bathroom, I had laid out silk boxers, a pair of black jeans, and a gold-colored T-shirt for him to wear. He sniffed the air once more. "Smells good. Sweet and sour meatballs, right?"

"Actually, today, I call them Royal Hawaiian Meat Balls." I grinned at him.

"Uh oh. What are you up to?"

He knew me all right. He willingly let me blindfold him and lead him to the table. I got him to sit down and draped his new royal blue robe over his shoulders. I set a gold-colored paper crown on his head, tucking a still-wet black curl beneath the gilded paper. I have to say he looked sexier still. I repositioned the tall candelabra a bit farther from him. "What's burning?" he asked.

"Don't worry, it's not your dinner," I said, and flicked on the cassette player. I had appropriated a marching tune of my dad's. It would have to do.

I whisked the blindfold off his face, and by the time his eyes had adjusted, I was holding a mirror in front of him. "Stuart, my love. This is your birthday. It had to be celebrated today."

He tilted his head from side to side, admiring the crown, and laughed. The flame of the candlelight shimmered, and its reflection sparkled in Stuart's blue eyes. He rose. "If my lady will excuse me, I shall return forthwith."

In a moment he returned and kneeled at my feet. "Every king needs a queen." He slipped a paper ring on the third finger of my left hand. "Will you marry me?"

I used the extra hour his boss had allowed him to show him I would.

Take it from this chef: Sometimes, the best men are so conscientious about carrying through on the commitments they undertake, it takes them a bit longer to pledge themselves to love and honor forever. The sizzle is worth the wait.

LORRAINE COYLE

♥ *Chef Tips* ♥

1. "Gold" paper crowns can be found at a well-known fast food chain or a party supply store.

2. Chef can be male, by adjusting the menu to reflect the coronation ceremony.

Tailgate
Mystery Date

 Preparation
Time

Moderate

 Cost

$

 Chef

Male or Female

---

*This would work well for any couple who has been
together for a while. It's sure to show your lover that
you want to "keep on keeping on."*

Ingredients

Favorite overstuffed sandwich

Favorite side dishes

Favorite beverage and bottle opener

Portable radio

*Glassware, plates, utensils, napkins, tablecloth or
blanket, candles or lanterns*

$\mathcal{M}$Y HUSBAND SWAGGERED through
the front door with his arm out-
stretched. "Get a load of this," he
gloated, one eyebrow lifted high. I didn't need to see the
envelope in his hand: I was the one who had sent it. I
opened the note anyway.

I KNOW WHAT YOU LIKE AND I HAVE
WHAT YOU WANT. INTERESTED?
FOLLOW THE ENCLOSED MAP. YOU'LL
NEED 45 MINUTES TRAVEL TIME.
MEET ME AT 8:00 P.M. FRIDAY.

Your Secret Admirer

"Hmm. She sure is confident about this. Are you going to go?" I asked, then turned away to mask my grin. I was relieved my husband was honest enough to show me the note, but I wondered now if my plan would work.

"Only if you don't mind, Sweet Cheeks. I sure would like to get to the bottom of this."

Andy and I have been married for twenty-five years. Romance and spontaneity had given way to comfortable companionship. Although I loved the trust-filled, secure relationship we had developed, I missed the passion of our early marriage. It was a risk, but I decided to try to rekindle the fire by becoming a mysterious admirer.

Intermittently over the previous few months, I had been sending candy, cigars, and small gifts. Anonymously, of course. At first, Andy shrugged off the gestures without a word. It made me nervous when he didn't mention them, but when I began sending notes with personal information, he took them seriously and showed them to me. Finally, it was time to reveal myself.

The Friday weather forecast promised to be mild and clear. I spent the afternoon preparing Andy's favorite outdoor repast—peppered roast beef and braised onion sandwiches on toasted garlic bread, pickled beets, deviled eggs, German potato salad, and chilled dark ale. I smiled as I remembered the first time we had shared this menu. He was playing quarterback for our college team and scored the winning goal. After the game we'd eaten our victory picnic on the fifty-yard line.

I tossed the picnic basket into the back of the car along with a couple of blankets, a lantern, and a battery-powered radio. The map I had provided Andy should delay him by fifteen minutes—long enough to allow me to set up the tailgate dinner.

When I arrived at the designated spot, I was devastated. There, in the spot where we had shared our first kiss so many years ago, was a blanket laid out with softly glowing candles and a bucket holding a chilled bottle of wine. "My favorite brand, too," I pouted. The soft music that drifted over the evening breeze obscured the sound of footsteps behind me.

"Hey there, Sweet Cheeks. Would you like to dance?" Andy had known it was me all along.

"Darn! I knew I couldn't fool you." I looked up into his shining eyes.

We danced and ate, then danced some more. We found a radio station that played oldies and cuddled, side by side, under the warm blanket. We counted the stars in the onyx sky. Instead of making wishes, we counted our blessings. In between soft kisses, we whispered the reasons we married each other. It wasn't long before the small flame of passion reminded us that we still needed and desired one another.

"By the way, the answer is 'yes.'" Andy whispered in my neck.

"'Yes,' what?" I pulled away slightly to look into the face I loved so well.

"The note from my secret admirer said she knows what I like and asked me if I was interested. I think you can tell that I am." He winked in the candlelight.

"Hmmm," I pulled the blanket over our heads, "then let me show you what she knows."

We laughed and loved all through the evening—and long into morning.

GAIL WOODS THOMPSON

❤ *Chef Tips* ❤

1. Choose a menu that is easy and portable. The atmosphere of the date will be enhanced if the food choices have a romantic "history" with the couple.
2. A tent would enhance the privacy factor.

Aunt Rita's Sugar Cookies

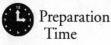
Preparation
Time
Fast

Cost
$

Chef
Male or Female

---

*A fancy date gone awry makes for a
warm family recipe.*

Ingredients

Loving concern

A sweetheart worth keeping

A planned date

I T ' S   N O T   A L W A Y S   E A S Y to date when you have
two kids, but Ron seemed to fit right in with our
family, never minding that sometimes I was late
because ballet practice ran over or had to go home early
when a fever struck. But this night was just for him—a
man does not turn thirty-five every day.

We planned for a Broadway show with dinner afterwards at an exclusive supper club restaurant. The kids
were going to spend the weekend with Great Aunt Rita,
an annual event they loved, which included popcorn,
videos, and making Aunt Rita's sugar cookies for the
annual church Christmas cookie exchange.

Aunt Rita's cookies were famous for the whimsical shapes she lovingly cut and decorated each year—reindeer and unicorns, pinwheels and wishing wands, castles and stars. Though asked many times for her secret, Auntie just smiles. "Love, my dear, is the special magic in my cookies. Love and nothing else."

As our special night arrived, everything was in place—my dress, his tux, Auntie's recipe, and the two giggling children who are the heart and soul of my life. We rang the doorbell on Auntie's front porch as anticipation sparkled in Ron's gaze, warming me past the slight chill in the air. He squeezed my hand.

It took a long moment before I realized Auntie was not going to answer the door. I dug in my evening bag for the key. She's probably just in the kitchen, I told myself as we entered the darkened hallway.

"Aunt Rita?" I called. My concern echoed unanswered through the house.

"Auntie, are you here?" Perhaps she'd gone to the store for last minute ingredients. But at eighty-seven, she rarely drove this late in the day.

Ron switched on the light as he and the children followed me into the house. His voice was soothing as he spoke to the children, though the glance he locked with mine mirrored my unspoken worries.

"Elizabeth?" Aunt Rita's quavering answer whispered from the front parlor. "What time is it?"

Relief flooded me, mixed with further concern. She was here, but she did not sound at all herself.

"Come on, kids," Ron said. "Let's see if your aunt has any hot chocolate in the kitchen."

Bless him, the man has a gift for knowing just how to ease an uncertain situation and shield the children at the same time.

With a nod, he ushered them down the hall as I entered the parlor. Aunt Rita lay on the sofa, pale and drawn in the artificial glow of the overhead light. She looked every one of those eighty-seven years.

"Auntie, you're ill." I told her stupidly, amazed at the depth of my surprise and dismay. My aunt was never ill or, at least, so it had seemed for most of my thirty years.

Her gaze ran over my evening gown and the upswept curl of my hair.

"Your night out." She struggled to sit up. "Oh, my dear, I'd forgotten."

The giggles of the children echoed down the hall. She raised a tremulous hand to her lips. "The cookie exchange. For the first time in seventy years I've let the church and the children down.

"I was going to the store this morning, but I was so tired I just lay down for a few minutes." Her voice trailed off and I touched her forehead. She was warm, but not overly feverish. Poor Ron. So much for our special celebration.

"You lie back down, Auntie." I told her when she started to stand. "And don't fret. I'll get you a cool drink."

"But your evening—"

"Our plans aren't anything we can't do another time." I covered her with an afghan and kissed her cheek. "I'll be right back."

The sight that greeted me as I entered the kitchen pushed all my concerns aside. Ron stood in the center of

Aunt Rita's kitchen with her best blue gingham apron tied about his waist. His tuxedo coat draped in casual elegance from the back of an antique chair. They'd dug out all the cookie cutters and Auntie's special cookie-making bowl. The children framed him with happy faces as the three of them bent over a recipe box, studying intently.

He looked up with a smile that warmed me to my toes. "The keys are on the counter. We made a list of ingredients we couldn't find. How's Rita?" Concern edged the gaze he locked with mine.

"Worried about ruining your evening." I said over the lump in my throat. "I think she has a touch of the flu. She just needs some aspirin and chicken soup and a little more rest."

"Well, kids." He put an arm around each. "I guess your family's cookie exchange tradition is up to us this year. Think we can handle it?"

Their enthusiastic endorsements rang through the room as they hugged him. So long Broadway and Ron's birthday. Would he ever forgive me?

"How are you?" I mouthed as I joined them.

"Terrific." He whispered catching my lips in a quick kiss. "The best birthdays are the ones made with love, my dear Elizabeth. Love and nothing else."

ELIZABETH KEYS

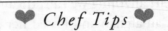

♥ *Chef Tips* ♥

1. Expect the unexpected.
2. Go with the flow.

One Hot Fajita

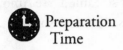 Preparation Time

Fast

 Cost

$

Chef

Male

This recipe instructs the reader in how to rustle up
a meal when time is of the essence and still be cool.

Ingredients

Tortillas

Mixed vegetables

Chicken or beef

Hot sauce

Cerveza

I WAS ON A BUSINESS TRIP to Mexico when I met her. Her name was Consuelo and she was in charge of arranging my stay in Acapulco and introducing me to my company's Mexican counterparts at the annual sales meeting. She was sexy and beautiful with long black hair, eyes like liquid chocolate, and a body the god Quetzalcoátl would have sacrificed someone for. Within five minutes of laying eyes on her, I was smitten.

Even though her English wasn't very good and my Spanish nonexistent, the soft touch of her hand and brush of her body required no translation. Soon all I could hear was "Consuelo, Consuelo, Consuelo" rattling inside my head like a bouncing beach ball. How could a mere mortal such as myself ever hope to invite the favors of such Latino perfection? For while my heart screamed "Te Amo, Te Amo, Te Amo," all I could say was, "So, Consuelo . . . another glass of champagne?"

The following Friday she suggested a group of us go to a local hangout after work. The place was hopping and, after a couple of drinks, I took my best shot.

"You hungry?" I asked.

"Starving," she replied.

"How'd you like me to cook us dinner at my place?"

Smiling brightly, she nodded and excused herself to the ladies room. Then things started to get a little weird. On her way back, a young man intercepted her and began arguing with her. An irate former boyfriend? I wondered. Worse, an irate current boyfriend? The last thing I wanted was to risk a bar fight in a country whose jails don't even come equipped with StairMasters.™

Much to my relief, Consuelo suggested we leave, and no sooner had we reached the sideway than a black sedan pulled up. Consuelo motioned for me to get into the front seat alongside her. My relief was short-lived, however, when I noticed that sitting in the back seat was the young man Consuelo had argued with. Worse, he had a gun in his lap. "O-my-god! " I said, as we sped off.

My company had put me up on the outskirts of town at a small villa owned by a man named Pepe, whose favorite expression, "Slow is fast enough, my friend," had become a local mantra. While there were rumors that the area was a known burying ground for Mexican mob kill, I had taken the rumors with a grain of salt—until now. How would it happen? I wondered. A bullet to the back of the head? Hung like a coconut from a palm tree? Images of Davy Crockett shooting it out at the Alamo filled my mind. As Consuelo squeezed my hand and smiled, my growing anxiety got the better of me. What if she's part of it? I could hear the dialogue clearly:

POLICE CAPTAIN
And you say the last time you saw him was at the Ticky-Tacky bar?
CONSUELO *(tears streaming down her face)*
My poor dead gringo. I told him not to drink the water.

Finally we arrived. I opened the car door, quickly jumped out, and ushered Consuelo inside. Turning around I saw the two men now standing in the doorway holding semi-automatic weapons. This was it—the moment of truth. Quetzalcoátl had returned for his piece of the action. That's when Consuelo began yelling at them in Spanish, and, as they yelled back, gesticulating with their raised guns, the absurdity of the situation pushed me over the edge.

I blurted out, "If you kill me, this beautiful young woman will starve to death!"

There was dead silence. Quizzically, Consuelo looked at me, translated what I'd said, and the three started laughing convulsively.

"They no kill you," she said. "These are my brothers. They here to protect my honor. They no believe you cook. They think you are up to no good."

"But . . . what about the guns?" I babbled.

"Oh, the guns," she said matter-of-factly, "they're Policia. They always carry guns. They're so overprotective."

"Well, if they promise to put the guns away, I'll cook for them too," I offered.

Then I was struck with a terror worse than a falling souffle: I had planned dinner for only two! Quickly I did a search and sort of my mental cookbook and realized that with a little tinkering, chicken in wine sauce with fresh vegetables for two could easily become sizzling chicken fajitas for four. Fortunately, Pepe had left some tortillas in the refrigerator and with fresh peppers, onions, and an improvised hot sauce, voilà!

Dinner was a complete success, and after lots of cerveza her brothers complimented me on the meal and left, comfortable in the knowledge that their sister was in good culinary hands.

Smiling from ear to ear, Consuelo proved the sweetest dessert imaginable as she held me in her arms, stroked my head, and whispered sweet nothings to me in Spanish.

"You know," I said, as we sat cuddling together on the couch, "that chicken truly sacrificed its life for me."

"You're lucky they didn't shoot you," she responded, nibbling on my ear.

"How so?" I inquired.

"They hate chicken."

ROBERT S. COHEN

❤ *Chef Tips* ❤

1. Don't be afraid to improvise when guests drop in.
2. Nothing goes as well with Mexican food as beer (cerveza).
3. Learn your date's native tongue and customs.

2.
RECIPES THAT COST LESS THAN $80

Those who give love, receive love.

– Frank Cabiroy

Stormy Weather in the Living Room

 Preparation Time

Long

 Cost

$$

 Chef

Male or Female

This is a date that is intended to spice up an evening.

Ingredients

Stormy weather CD (see Chef Tips for specific titles)

Candles

Fondue pot

Italian or French bread

Fondue with cheddar and Swiss cheeses and a half cup of beer

Apples, sliced

Partner's favorite beverage

Sixteen-ounce chocolate bar for melting

Fresh strawberries

Banana

Marshmallows

Flavored liqueur, 3 tablespoons

Strobe light (optional)

*T*HERE IS SOMETHING very romantic about a thunderstorm. The pounding of thunder, flashes of light against a dark backdrop, and the sound of water cascading off the windows creates such a wonderful ambiance. Even if it isn't raining, all of this can be obtained with a little technology and a lot of innovation.

One Saturday morning in July, my girlfriend, Carol, was called in to work. We'd spent the entire week looking forward to being together, so this ruined our plans. We'd hoped for a day at the beach followed by an evening of romance. I could see the dismal expression on her face as she got into her car and headed for work. I began to think—what can I do to surprise her and make up for our lost day? A clap of thunder in the distance gave me a wonderful idea.

Carol always found thunderstorms to be romantic. Well, there really isn't any way to guarantee a thunderstorm. Or is there? I went into my home and began looking through my CD collection. I found two CDs that would provide us with almost three hours of thunder and rain sound effects. Next I began to think about what we would do if we were really at the beach and it began to rain. I looked around my house and began to move all the furniture out of my living room and look for a blanket to place in the middle of the floor.

I created a marvelous fantasy: Carol and I are on an island. A storm arises and we have to find shelter. We find a place, but it is just a shack. There is no electricity, so we must use candles to illuminate our hut.

I set up the apartment as if it were a mere shelter. Around seven that evening, Carol arrived looking very tired. I put in the CD and lit several candles. As she entered, she heard the thunder and saw the reflection of the strobe I'd rented flashing on one of the walls. Her puzzled look lasted until she saw the candles, the blanket, and me—dressed in my bathing suit. She really wasn't in the mood for fantasy, and when I handed her a bikini she grumbled some. But I cajoled her until she went into the bathroom to change.

As she was getting dressed, I set up the cheese fondue on the blanket. She came out of the bathroom and smiled when she saw the fondue. I walked over to her and whispered, "Tonight it's just the two of us on a deserted island." I dipped a piece of bread in the cheese and held it to her mouth.

"I don't think so," she said, smiling. "That's much too large."

I chuckled. "I guess size does matter." I tore it in half, one bite for each of us. That shared taste—and the shoulder massage I gave her—put her day behind her so we could focus on each other.

"Mmmm," she hummed. "That really helps." For a while silence fell. "Deserted island?"

"Yeah."

"Nice." Another pause. "We have to eat all this food ourselves?"

"Right," I said, and took the opportunity to sneak a kiss. She laughed with delight. "Let's get started."

We fed each other dipped bread and apple slices until all the cheese was gone. She curled up in my arms, and we sat on the blanket and listened to the rain. I kissed her on the forehead and said, "I love you with all my heart."

She smiled. "This is even better than the beach. And I love you, too." For the rest of the evening we felt like we really were the only two people in the world.

After a while I got up to put the empty fondue pot in the kitchen and came back with another pot filled with melted chocolate and blackberry brandy. Her face lit up like that strobe light. She loves chocolate. I went back for a plate of marshmallows, fresh strawberries, and chopped banana chunks. Once again we fed each other. In our eagerness between CD thunderbolts, we spilled a fair amount of chocolate. Naturally we had to kiss the splashes all over our faces and elsewhere off. Passion and chocolate. Delicious.

I was happy that we never made it to the real beach. Our night together was perfect. We laughed, ate, held each other, and let the thunder roll.

MICHAEL MATTEO

❤ *Chef Tips* ❤

1. The CDs that I used were: *Relaxing With Nature— Thunderstorm/Raindrops* produced by Distributions Madacy Inc. and *Nature's Symphonies: Midnight Storm* by Delta Music Inc.
2. If you choose to use a strobe light, make sure that it has a long enough delay so that it is not flickering so quickly that it hurts your eyes.
3. The cheese and chocolate fondues are just things that we like to eat. There are many fondue recipe books, and I suggest choosing your lover's favorite foods to create your own fondue.
4. Choose a beverage that fits the island theme: Daiquiris, Strawberry Colada, etc.

Soft Center Special

 Preparation Time
Moderate

💰 Cost
$$

👨‍🍳 Chef
Male

For the regretful man who's got something to prove.

Ingredients

Cuddly toy

Crab

Marshmallows

Soft-centered chocolates

I WAS AT THE club dancing with Mike when I saw Greg. I hadn't seen him in years, yet my heart lurched. I wanted to run over and throw my arms around his neck. Instead, I went home. Instead of sleeping, I lay remembering how Greg and I had grown up together. We'd been the best of buddies. When we were eight, I'd decided I was going to marry him, but when we were sixteen, everything went wrong.

Greg's parents split up, and he got angry and joined the wrong crowd. It wasn't long before he quit school and got into minor trouble with the law and started drinking heavily. I tried to see him, but he always pushed me away. It hurt, but mostly I was frightened for Greg, for where he was going.

About a year later, I went to see him. I stood in the filthy little room he lived in and wanted to weep. I'd had a big speech planned, but all I could say was, "I love you, Greg. Please come home."

He erupted. Told me to get out of his life and stay out. That he wasn't the soft little kid that he used to be and I made him sick. He said a lot of other things too, and he broke my heart. Worst of all was walking away and knowing that it was a hard-faced stranger I was leaving behind.

I wondered where my buddy, the Greg who'd picked me wildflowers for my fourteenth birthday, who had once spent three hours rescuing a trapped kitten, had gone?

The morning after I'd seen him at the club, I somehow wasn't surprised when the phone rang before it was even daylight. A great, gut-wrenching longing flooded through me as I heard Greg's voice, just as it had when I was a teenager.

"Ali, I'd like to see you," he said.

But all I could hear were his long-ago words to me. I said no, even though it hurt.

"Please," he begged, and I gave in and agreed to go to his house for supper that night. I figured that once I saw him again and realized that he really wasn't the Greg I'd grown up with, then maybe, I'd finally get over him. Maybe then, I'd be able to get on with my life. Maybe now, I could finally leave him and my childhood behind.

I was nervous when I rang his bell, and when he opened the door, I couldn't think of a thing to say. He looked so good. Fit and healthy with his dark hair brushed back and his blue eyes clear.

"Ali. You look wonderful. Come in," he said, and led the way to his living room where a fire flickered in a grate, the sofa was soft with cushions, and the table was set with candles and flowers.

Wildflowers. My heart did a little skip in my chest.

We sat on the couch and talked for a while. He told me he'd gotten out of the crowd he'd been running with and was in construction and doing okay for himself. He seemed nervous, and he jumped up and handed me a parcel. Inside was a goofy-faced stuffed toy—a cat, and goose bumps shivered up my spine. I didn't know what to say. Wildflowers and a cat . . . Was it possible Greg was doing this deliberately? As if he knew I needed a few minutes to myself, he said, "I'll get supper ready." He raced out and came back with a big bowl and put it on the hearth.

"I thought we could toast marshmallows later."

I shrugged. It seemed a strange choice for a supper, but then again, why not? We'd done it often enough as kids. Hold on—wildflowers, a cat, and marshmallows . . . What was he up to? Before I could make sense of it, Greg went out and came back with the rest of the supper.

As he set it on the table, he said, "I got crab, because it might have a hard shell on the outside, but it's sweet and soft inside, and the chocolates," he picked one up and opened the paper, broke it in half, "are all soft-center, too."

My heart started to pound. There were a lot of not-very-subtle messages here. "Greg," I said. "What's all this about?"

He came and stood by the fire, jammed his fists into the pockets of his jeans. "I know it was probably kind of stupid," he said, "but I wanted to remind you of what we used to have before I hurt you, and I want a chance to prove to you that I'm still the same person I was, deep inside. Ali . . ." he stared deep into my eyes, and at the expression I saw in his, all my old hopes, all my love for him rose up in a great wave.

"For three years," he said, "I've been too proud to say sorry. But Ali, I am. More sorry than I can say. I don't expect you to forgive me, just like that," he snapped his fingers, "but I'm hoping that maybe we can be friends again." He reached for me, and his hands trembled as he drew me to my feet. What he said next took my breath away.

"Ali," he said, "I want to come home."

And I tumbled, willingly, into his arms.

We never quite got to eat the marshmallows, but I didn't care. Nothing could have been as sweet and soft as the kisses we shared.

SUE EMMS

💙 *Chef Tips* 💙

1. Find gifts and settings that bring back good memories.

2. Practice the apology, so you get it right.

3. Remember that it usually takes time as well as spoken regrets to find your way "home."

Power Play

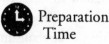 Preparation
Time
Moderate

 Cost
$$

 Chef
Female

*An end-around run to make sure the sportsman of
your dreams remembers the real rules in the
Super Bowl of Romance.*

Ingredients

Masking tape

Suitable music

Team jersey and helmet (optional)

DESPERATE TIMES demand desperate
measures. I never really knew what that
phrase meant until I met Michael.

Michael is the ultimate sports fanatic. He breathes fire
when he thinks of athletic competition. He paws at the
ground and beats his chest. To me it might have been a
den, but it was his dugout, his spot on the scrimmage line
of life. After dating for a while, I could tell he was just
waiting for the day when the hockey puck would come
flying out of the television set and smash into his jaw.

I should have known I'd have some stiff competition

for his affection the day we met. He introduced himself by saying, "Hi, I'm a systems analyst and a left-handed reliever with an 8-2 record, 10 saves this season, and 50 career wins." But he was cute, blond hair with curls that had minds of their own and the kind of eyes that capture you and won't let go. He was also wearing a baseball uniform, a little tight in the right places if you know what I mean. Besides, the first time I let one of those golden ringlets slide across the back of my hand I was a goner, so I decided to work with the sports references for a while and see what happened.

I became a runner, a rower, and a volleyball player. I learned all the NBA teams by uniform color, home and away, and could recite the starting lineup for every World Series game for the past ten years. So what was the problem, you ask?

Because Michael's pet name for me was "the Babe" (I was flattered until I remembered about that Ruth guy who played for the Yankees), I made the mistake of thinking I had the sports-thing down pat and was more exciting than Michael Jordan doing a perfect lay-up in a double team with a minute left in the game, score tied. One evening I said to him, "Honey, tonight it's either me or the Bulls." The next thing I heard sounded strangely like my hair dryer hitting the sidewalk.

So now it was sudden death overtime: one chance to win him back with the clock running and no time-outs.

I called Michael and asked him to come over and explain a few hockey rules I didn't quite understand, like the concept of icing. He couldn't resist. I had an hour to get ready.

I divided the living room rug into the sections of a hockey rink, marked out a goal crease in front of the sofa with masking tape, and put on the soft refrains of "Jock Rock 3." As the CD player crooned "We Will, We Will, Rock You," I lowered the house lights, donned my secret weapon, and waited.

The doorbell rang. My heart pounded as I walked to the door. I dipped my head, felt everything fall into place, and pulled the door open. There I stood, in a New Jersey Devil's hockey jersey and goalie mask.

And absolutely nothing else.

For a long moment Michael just stared at me. Then one of those beautiful smiles I'd come to know curled his lips. "Honey, what's this?" His stunning blue eyes examined my outfit from the top of my head to the tips of my toes with obvious appreciation.

"If you can't beat them, join them," I said, pulling him inside. "I want to make sure I'm still in the game."

Michael reached out and lifted the mask from my face. "If I made you think something else, I'm sorry. You know you mean more to me than anything," he said, right before crushing his mouth to mine.

"I can share you with the Bulls, the Giants, the Devils, and the Mets," I replied, leading him to the sofa. "But I want you to know that halftime, between periods, and the seventh inning stretch belong to me."

"That's fair enough," Michael said, chuckling. Just as the "Hey" song, the tune the New Jersey Devils use when they score, came on the stereo, he noticed the unique floor marking and burst out laughing. "Looks like we're both in the crease," he said, snaking his arms around me and cupping my backside with his hands. "Doesn't that negate the score?"

"I think the official scorer would allow the goal this time," I replied as he nibbled my neck. "But it appears as though you're in the process of checking from behind," I continued as his hands moved in sensuous massage across my back, bottom, and thighs. "I could argue a penalty, but this is one personal foul I really like."

Laughing, Michael kissed me again, and together we tumbled onto the couch to begin the first of many championship seasons in each other's arms.

KATHRYN QUICK

❤ *Chef Tips* ❤

1. If you go for the team jersey option, be careful not to choose one your sportsman really dislikes; it could destroy the mood. You're usually safe using the current winners of the Super Bowl, the World Series, the Stanley Cup, or the NBA Championship.

2. For obvious reasons, do not give in to the temptation of using real chalk to make the yard-line markers on your rug.

3. Most important of all, approach this type of situation with patience and understanding. After all, sportsmen need love, too.

Late Christmas Dinner Surprise

 Preparation Time

Long

Cost

$$

Chef

Male or Female

The recipe will show the taster that love really exists and that it can happen quickly, even if the past has shown something different.

Ingredients

Secret note pad

Blindfold

Items necessary to recreate a holiday, in this case Christmas:

Eggnog	Cinnamon potpourri
Christmas music	Christmas tree
Poinsettias	Fireplace
Candy canes	Gingerbread house

CHRISTIE AND I were friends at first—bonded by broken hearts refusing to rebound. We were convinced true love did not exist.

As friends, we talked about anything and everything.

One day I remember telling her, "Too many people love the idea of being in love and aren't really in love with a person, especially when it happens too quickly. You really need to get to know someone well before you claim you love them."

She agreed and said, "I think people mistake convenience for love. It's convenient to have someone who keeps you company and gives you security. But I don't think that's a reason to love someone. I personally want someone who loves me, not loves the way I make him feel."

Within months of our conversation, I was having a hard time admitting that Christie was everything I'd ever hoped for. She was passionate about everything she did—studying, smiling, and being my best friend. Different from others, her sky blue eyes gave me the feeling that my heart would be safe in her hands—a feeling I had never felt.

I began falling in love with her, and it was not because I needed good company. I had played that game already and, frankly, I preferred being alone over "loving someone" just for the sake of "loving anyone." But of course I knew I'd feel like a hypocrite if I merely told her, so I decided to show her.

I kept my feelings to myself for a month or so, and then I planned the most creative date I could think of while I was on Christmas break visiting my family. My Christie deserved the best I had to offer, and I wanted her to know it. I wanted to give her a date that would let her now that I *was* falling in love with her. I also needed time to be sure love caused my burning and not some false feeling in disguise.

For starters, I returned early from Christmas break. I arrived two days before she did, so I could make the necessary arrangements. Then I met her at the airport with the most beautiful red roses I could find.

Her expression engraved itself on my mind. She said nothing, but her eyes told me everything I needed to know.

We embraced and I whispered to her, "I'm kidnapping you for the day because I've got to show you something important."

She looked uncertain, but she agreed anyway.

We drove to a nearby state park. I blindfolded her with a burgundy velvet cloth. She felt its soft sheen and smiled—velvet was her favorite. I led her out of the car and down a woodchip-strewn path, opened the door to the cabin I had rented, and guided her in.

"Ummm! Cinnamon potpourri! I love that smell . . . it says 'Christmas' to me," she said. "But aren't you a little late? Didn't Christmas already happen?"

That set up my surprise beautifully. I picked up the remote control and hit play on the CD player. Then I removed the velvet blindfold.

Her face glowed like a child's at the sight of Christmas presents on Christmas morning. She looked around the room, calling out all the things she noticed.

"A natural Christmas tree! Poinsettias everywhere! Presents! A gingerbread house! Eggnog! A fireplace! And it smells like you cooked something! Oh, you're playing the Trans Siberian Orchestra's Christmas album!"

I just smiled.

"I love that album," she said, as she began laughing.

"How did you remember I liked all these things? I casually mentioned it once . . . I think! I don't think even my parents could have planned this!"

"Well, I am a college student," I said to her, "In college we take lots of notes, so you could say I am addicted to note taking.

"The truth is I began taking notes on everything you mentioned that you liked. I knew you wouldn't just take my word for it so here it is . . . PROOF! Proof that I am really in love with you . . . not just anybody . . . I am in love with Christie ."

"Really?"

"I am crazy about you . . . you wanna see?" I asked. I ran out of the cabin to the nearby lake and, as loud as I could, I screamed "I LOVE CHRISTIE!!!!" and let it echo back across the water.

She followed me outside and opened her arms, inviting me into her embrace. She hugged me tighter than ever and said, "I believe you."

She placed her hands on my cheeks and brought my face closer to hers. I could feel her breath on my lips just before we kissed for the first time.

I leaned back just far enough to look into her eyes and said to her, "This is my first Christmas with the woman I hope to spend all the rest of my Christmases with. You are the one for me, Christie. I hope I am the one for you."

We walked back toward the cabin, our arms around each other, and I told her, "I even learned to cook. Took me forever, burned some pots and pans, but it was worth it. I cooked *our* dinner."

She smiled, kissed me again, and said, "Christmas is the season I always dreamed of getting married in . . . you may want to make a note of that!"

MARIO I. OÑA

❤ *Chef Tips* ❤

1. If you are going to surprise someone by returning early, make sure the person you plan to surprise will be there.

2. Feel free to use any holiday. The idea is to bring back something that may otherwise be lost forever. As the aphorism suggests: "Better late than never."

3. The cost depends partly on the holiday you want to reenact.

4. Subtly take notes of things your potential love says he or she likes. You'll be amazed at how easy getting a present or preparing a surprise will be if you do this.

New Year's Eve, Alone Together

 Preparation
Time

Long

$ Cost

$$

Chef

Male or Female

---

*Sharing cherished memories and secret fantasies
of the future will reopen neglected avenues of
communication and refresh romance.*

Ingredients

Candlelight and one good reading lamp

Cushions for two

Coffee table

Large tablecloth

Two place settings of your best china and silver

Flowers

Two champagne flutes

A bottle or two of good bubbly

Picnic take-out dinner

Handsome calendar/journal for the coming year

THE New Year's Eve date! So much anticipation. So little real excitement. Frozen extremities and claustrophobia in Times Square. Over-priced dinner and dancing in sequins and black tie among a surfeit of stiff strangers. Honeymoon intimacy, pink champagne, and charred filet mignon. One babysitter, six neighbors, twelve hats and horns, and two decks of cards.

And suddenly, we'd been married for fifteen years, and the new year had sneaked up on us again. As we weeded through the debris of a good Christmas, I felt as though we ought to be doing something important, something romantic this year.

"What do you want to do New Year's Eve?" I asked, arranging Christmas garlands in a storage box.

"I dunno. What do you want to do?"

"Well, we could—"

"Too expensive."

"How about—?"

"Too loud and crowded."

"Okay, then—"

"Boring."

After fifteen years, we can read each other's minds. It's a blessing and a curse, especially when both compartments are musty and cobweb ridden.

"We could ignore it," I offered.

"You can't ignore New Year's Eve."

With an I-give-up sigh, I glanced down at the book in my hand. An unclaimed Christmas present from an uninspired relative or business associate? A calendar/journal for the coming year bound in burgundy leather. Handsome, but essentially useless: we have no time in our lives for waxing nostalgic, enshrining memories, or planning beyond quick notes on a wall calendar.

Just look at the yawning void where our New Year's Eve plans should be. Except for a date book and the germ of an idea.

"What would you think about—"

♥

At seven P.M. on New Year's Eve, Tom returned from a three hour no-holds-barred-go-for-broke exotic, all-American-male gourmet and junk food foray, arms loaded with a bottle of good champagne, another of Chardonnay—we'd flipped a coin and decided we'd both won—and a clumsy but fragrant picnic of our favorite take-out finger foods. While he showered and slipped into his favorite sweater and jeans, I floated a gold table cloth over the coffee table, allowed it to pool on the floor like one of Salome's veils, and set out two place settings of our best silver and china and two crystal champagne flutes. Instead of cramming the flowers Tom had brought into a vase, I scattered them on the table. I'd already transformed myself into an alluring sylph in silk evening pajamas left-over from the fantasy lifestyle of some long-forgotten year.

Tom got a crackling fire going in the hearth and arranged an assortment of cushions and pillows into comfortable floor seating while I sorted out the shrimp and cocktail sauce, crab cakes, mini-racks of ribs, roast beef on mini-challah rolls, lobster salad and croissants, chili dogs, crudités/fruit/cheese platter, Ritz crackers/peanut butter/jelly, slices of meatloaf on country white, ramekins of mac and cheddar, and more. Dessert would be a "dessert cart" of mousse in chocolate shells, fruit and nut tarts, chocolate cake, French/Italian pastries, and triple fudge brownies. All in all, a veritable his and hers, child and gourmet buffet of comfort and adventure. Perfect for New Year's Eve feasting and sharing.

Candlelight and "our music" did a marvelous job of blurring the edges of everyday life and smoothing out the wrinkles of passing time. The Tom Jones style finger-licking, lip-sharing buffet seduced us away from the present into a free-floating mist of past and present.

Tom poured our wine, and we raised our glasses to toast the good fortune of our life together—family, home, careers, and each other. Beneath the stress and hassle of everyday life, we were among the blessed and lucky where it counted most.

Including memories.

"Remember what we used to do on New Year's Day before the kids came along?"

"Late church. Coffee and donuts to go. A walk on the beach."

"Think the kids are old enough?" Tom reached for the leather diary that had prompted our New Year's Eve date with ourselves.

"Put it on the calendar. And our old first Sunday of the month date?"

"Pancakes and tunes at the Broadway diner? Still sounds good," he decided, scribbling quickly, while I nibbled on a shrimp and then his ear. Tom eyed me with a wary stare. "Does this mean no NFL playoffs games or Super Bowl on TV?"

"Not as long as you're free by February when the couples tennis lessons start."

"Deal," he agreed, flipping to the next calendar page. "You know what I miss? Our midnight Friday R-rated video dates," he said, answering his own question.

"You're tired of Disney? Me, too. And I know you miss the sailboat." We'd sold the racing skiff when the kids came along—too time consuming, too expensive. "The kids are old enough for River Rats sailing lessons and an occasional Sunday afternoon without us. Picnics on the river at sunset," I fantasized.

"Races at the boat club," Tom mused.

We debated the subject over ribs and roast beef before compromising with a kiss and moving on—to the summer.

The pen scribbled on, changing the face of the coming year.

"What do you want for your birthday?" Tom asked with a sample offer of nibbling kisses and a bone-melting backrub.

"More of this, a good camera, a summer of Saturdays exploring all the places we haven't been to in years, and each other," I whispered. "What would you like for your birthday?

"Hot stuff. A balloon ride, hang gliding, and you."

We were only up to September and 11:00 P.M. New Year's Eve, but I thought we had this fantasy stuff figured out well enough to take a short break from writing it down. Especially since the candles were guttering out, the fire fading to black, and our imaginations on full sensory alert.

PATRICIA LEARY

❤ *Chef Tips* ❤

1. The cost is greater if the beverage is vintage champagne.

2. New Year's Eve can be a perfect time for looking back and looking ahead. Even wonderful marriages need to change as life changes. During the middle years, most of us focus on family needs and goals. Our needs as individuals or as a couple tend to be put aside while the children are growing up. Writing down those dates with each other make it less likely opportunities will be lost in the shuffle of everyday life.

3. The leather calendar/journal becomes a cherished keepsake, especially when you take the time to record the best bits of your adventures.

One Less Angel

🕛 Preparation
Time
Moderate

💰 Cost
$$

👨‍🍳 Chef
Male

A memory to last a lifetime (and then some).

Ingredients

Conviction

Eggnog with rum or equivalent

Horse and buggy or equivalent

One diamond engagement ring

I T WASN'T THAT I didn't love Maryann. I loved her very much. It was just . . . well, you know: the "C" word. For guys, Commitment is genetically linked to fear—like sex and headaches in women. Or perhaps I was experiencing anxiety as a result of my first marriage—which ended abruptly when my wife, Darlene, mistook me for a rump roast and tried to slice and dice me with an eight-inch carving knife.

Not wishing to go down without a healthy fight, I diligently perused my well-worn copy of *The Single Guy's*

Lexicon of Delaying Tactics, finding such stellar examples as "My therapist thought it might be counterproductive to make a commitment to anyone but him/her at this time," "I'm waiting to pay off my student loan so we can afford a house," and the ever popular "I need time to get in touch with my inner self." All was lost, however, when Maryann outflanked me with "You have a choice: either marry me, or I'm outta here."

The sheer simplicity of her logic was hard to refute. And so, finding myself like a pig on a skewer, I responded equivocally. "Uh . . . would you mind if I took some time to think about it?" I said.

Women are dangerous when they employ logic and, if Maryann was anything, she was logical. She was unlike any woman I had ever gone out with—intelligent, responsible, faithful, reliable, conscientious, as well as cute, sexy, and a great kisser. For a guy working in the theater whose dating universe was largely populated with women whose mental state bordered on schizophrenic, it was a refreshing change. So, knowing that I loved her more than anything else in the world and didn't want to risk losing her, I decided it was time.

As luck would have it, it was just nearing the Christmas season, and every year Maryann ordered tickets for her father, sister, niece, and us to go to her favorite event: Midnight Mass at St. Patrick's Cathedral in New York—a spectacular ceremony, broadcast nationally, which employed a full symphony orchestra, chorus, and soloists from the Metropolitan Opera. All in all, a perfectly public place for a guy with a dramatic flair to propose marriage. Of course, I wasn't about to propose in front of her family.

Fortunately, they'd always find an excuse to punk out at the last minute, leaving Maryann and me to go alone. Just in case, I planned to triple the amount of rum I put in the eggnog—they were going nowhere. Everything was set: the tickets, the diamond ring, even a hansom cab to meet us in front of the cathedral after the service.

Finally the moment arrived. As we sat in St. Patrick's along with a thousand or so other people—and more angels than could fit on the head of a pin—I fumbled in my pocket for the ring. She must have figured something was up because she got that "Oh, no—not here" look after spotting a small rivulet of fluid forming on the floor beneath my sweating hands. On cue, at the stroke of midnight, St. Patrick's was awash in white flood lights as the cameras rolled, the orchestra played, and the choir began singing "Oh, Come All Ye Faithful," just as I had planned.

As everyone stood, I turned to Maryann, took out the ring, and said, "Of all the angels here tonight, none are as beautiful as you. Will you marry me?"

A momentary look of shock crossed her face as she blurted out, "I can't believe you're doing it here," followed by "Yes, yes . . . oh, yes."

Those close enough to see what was going on smiled and shook our hands just as Cardinal O'Conner came up the aisle swinging the burning frankincense and myrrh. As he passed by, I'm sure I saw him wink. I couldn't have cast him in a better cameo role.

Several years after we were married, I obtained a video-tape of that evening's ceremony. Of course, in the sea of people we were nowhere to be seen, but if you look carefully at the beginning of the tape, you can see a small flash of light. Maryann thinks it's the floodlights reflecting off the ring. I think it's something else. I think it's the flash of one of the angels leaping off the head of that proverbial pin into my heart.

ROBERT S. COHEN

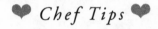

❤ *Chef Tips* ❤

1. Choose an event that brings her joy. It doesn't have to be big, just important to her.

2. Plan for contingencies—like weather, family, etc.

3. Personalize your proposal to the event.

4. It must be a total surprise, so pick a place she would never suspect.

5. Note that cost above does not include diamond ring.

Surprise Scavenger Hunt

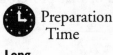 Preparation Time

Long

 Cost

$$

 Chef

Male or Female

This date is for someone with a fun-loving personality. It helps to keep a straight face, too.

Ingredients

Cowboy boots, red garter, and other accessories

Accomplice

ANTONIO'S BIRTHDAY was fast approaching, and I wanted to do something special for him, something he would remember for years to come. A surprise party was out of the question since he had already expressed an interest in spending an evening alone with me. But that was no reason he couldn't be surprised in another way!

I made up a strange list for a shopping spree and told Antonio that my uncle needed the items for some reason unbeknownst to me.

"Okay, what's our first stop?" he asked.

"Well, that's an easy one," I said. "The flea market."

As we strolled along the aisles of vendors selling their

trash and treasures, Antonio was visibly perplexed when I said, "These are perfect!" Antonio had no idea that I'd scoped the place out the day before and knew exactly where I'd find my first item on the list.

Now he stood there, mouth agape, while I proudly held up a pair of weather-beaten cowboy boots.

"Shelly, your uncle wants you to buy a pair of old cowboy boots?"

"That's what's on the list."

"Well, what size does he wear?"

"Eleven, I think."

"And what size are those?"

I knew this was going to take some creative thinking. "Looks like they're nines. But . . . he didn't tell me a specific size. Knowing Uncle Lloyd, he's probably using them as planters for his flowers."

Antonio rolled his eyes, while I forked over the five dollars to the vendor.

Next stop was an arts and crafts store. As I dragged Antonio through the rows of ribbons and silk flowers, I anticipated what his next reaction would be.

"Oh, here they are," I exclaimed happily. Again Antonio's face contorted into a puzzled expression as I made my selection from an array of plastic miniatures.

"That's what your uncle needs? A plastic tractor, cow, and farmer?"

I glanced again at my list, pretending to scrutinize it. "Uh-huh. Listed right here before the goat cheese and a red lace garter."

"What?!" Antonio said, taking the list from my hand to see for himself.

"We're almost done," I said, unable to resist a smile.

After making a stop at the local orchard market, which carried a full line of meats, dairy, fruits, vegetables, and a large assortment of homemade desserts, we were lucky enough to get the last package of goat cheese.

"Big seller, huh?" Antonio said, obviously amused by this entire shopping spree.

"Well, you can never have enough goat cheese, I guess." I gave him a playful kiss on the lips. "Maybe if you're lucky, Uncle Lloyd will share it with you."

"That's okay," Antonio said, trying to sniff the cheese through its wrapper. "Wouldn't want to deprive Uncle Lloyd of his favorite cheese. I'll just settle for the Swiss I have at home."

Though he didn't ask, I could tell he was wondering when Uncle Lloyd had taken an interest in goat cheese.

I had no trouble interesting Antonio in our last stop. The lingerie store carried a surprisingly large selection of lace garters, having several different styles in red.

"Why don't you choose it?" I told him. His face lit up at the suggestion.

"This one's nice," he said, picking out a garter that had a row of little faux diamond studs adorning its band.

"Well, it's getting late. We'd better get over to my uncle's house before he turns in."

Uncle Lloyd greeted us at the door and happily took the packages from my arms. Offering Antonio and me a seat in the living room, he went into the kitchen, then returned with two mugs of tea.

Conversation was wonderful and the time passed quickly. Before we knew it, it was nearly 11:30. A big night for Uncle Lloyd, as Antonio said on the way back to my house.

"So what's in the care package your uncle gave you?" Antonio asked. Uncle Lloyd had handed me a huge brown bag on our way out the door.

"Oh, just some goods he canned," I replied, trying to keep from laughing.

"Come in for a minute?" I asked casually, knowing Antonio would want us to spend some time alone before leaving.

"Why don't you go see what's on TV," I said, "while I put this away?"

Thankfully he didn't insist on helping. And it was all I could do to keep him from carrying the package as well. I knew he would surely have taken a peek inside if he had.

Going to work fast, I removed the items from Uncle Lloyd's care package—all of the items Antonio and I had bought.

Praying Antonio would busy himself with the television, I removed from the refrigerator a birthday cake that I had baked early that morning. Carefully I arranged the little plastic tractor, farmer, and cow. They looked great next to the inscription, "Happy Birthday, Cowboy." "Cowboy" was my nickname for Antonio, since he loved to play cowboy on his time off. And he always wore faded jeans, complete with western boots and hat.

Next I lined one of the leather cowboy boots with a plastic bag, filled it with water, and arranged a bouquet of fresh flowers that I'd also kept hidden in the refrigerator.

Finally, I slipped off the sneakers I'd been wearing all day and replaced them with a pair of high heels. As a finishing touch, I worked the red lace garter up my thigh to hide beneath my short skirt.

"Antonio," I called, while I lit the candles on his birthday cake. "Can you help me a minute?"

"There's nothing on telev. . . " his voice faded as he realized what I'd been up to all day.

"Happy birthday, honey," I said, finally able to release the laugh I'd been hiding all day.

"Today's not my birthday, it's . . . "

"After midnight," I said, "and it's now. Just very early!"

"I can't believe you did all this," he said and laughed. "And I can't believe Uncle Lloyd knew about this all along."

"Couldn't have done it without him," I said.

"Wait a minute," Antonio said, taking inventory of the items. "Where does the goat cheese come in?"

"Oh," I said, "that really was for Uncle Lloyd. There's a new recipe he wants to try."

"And the red garter?"

I smiled wickedly. "That would be yours. Now why don't you blow out the candles and make a wish."

"Honey, it's already come true. This is the best birthday I've ever had."

CHELLE MARTIN

❤ *Chef Tips* ❤

1. Decide on how much you want to spend before choosing your items for the list.
2. Base your items around something your loved one has an interest in, but don't make the connection too obvious.

Bicycle Built for Two

 Preparation Time
Long

$ Cost
$$

Chef
Male or Female

A personal and patriotic trip to a simpler day when a Small Town Fourth meant fun, friendship, community, and sharing. This date celebrates not only romance, but the true meaning of the holiday without the stress of traffic, travel, and superficial entertainment.

Ingredients

Traditional American small town

Bicycle built for two (rented)

Casual clothes suitable for biking

Calendar of holiday events from local newspaper, etc.

Camera and film

Reservations at a local diner

Lawn chairs, blanket, and picnic supper

Sunscreen and bug spray

JOE AND I had grown up together, played together, been high school sweethearts, and ultimately settled down to raise a family in the same small town. Before the nest emptied out, the Fourth of

July was Family Day with a huge barbecue in the afternoon and fireworks at night. Last week, Joe announced that the more things change, the more they stay the same—and the more they ought to change.

As I tried to puzzle that out, he announced, "I love you, but we are in a rut. Come with me and be my love for the holiday."

"Are you suggesting Xanadu and beds of roses with flags and bunting?"

"Not quite, but, yes, a bit of Norman Rockwell romance on wheels."

"I'd go anywhere with you, my love," I replied.

Which is why I wasn't totally surprised when my date for the day went temporarily missing in the early morning of the 4th of July, though I was a bit confused when he rang our doorbell and presented me with a nosegay of red, white, and blue carnations like a old-fashioned suitor.

"Your chariot awaits, my lady," he announced tipping his straw boater and setting its twin on my upswept hair.

"A bicycle?"

"Built for two. Rented."

"I haven't ridden anything but an exercise bike in years."

"Not to worry. It's like great sex: you never really forget. Believe me I know," he insisted with a wicked wink.

Laughing and wobbling along with a gentle "tail" breeze, we set off along our tree-lined street heading for the center of town.

"Where are we going?" I asked, when I dared to breathe.

"Breakfast of the best pancakes in the world."

For us, that meant the old-fashioned chrome diner a

block from Main Street. Dear, thoughtful man—he'd even reserved the same booth we'd shared on our very first official date: colas after a movie. He'd brought me a red rose that night, and one waited on my plate this morning. The endearing gesture was far sweeter than the blueberry pancakes and maple syrup that followed, almost as delicious as my "thank you" kiss and his "you're welcome" hug.

We continued our tour with a leisurely pedal along Main Street to admire how the town had rolled up the old sidewalks and replaced them with brick walkways, park benches, shade trees, and tubs of annuals exploding with color. We stopped to chat and joke with everyone who smiled our way: a young policeman, an awed toddler and her mom, shopkeepers just opening their doors.

"You still turn every head with just a smile," Joe whispered, sending me another flirtatious wink.

At the combination variety and hardware store, twenty-five years of married life kicked in as we simultaneously hit the brakes and dashed inside for kid-sized American flags, crepe paper streamers, and balloons. The four pre-adolescents staring at our bike when we returned accepted a share of the bounty in exchange for a refresher class in bike decorating. They sailed off in search of more swash-buckling adventure while we tooled along the avenue admiring the refurbished early twentieth century façades of the buildings we'd known for decades. Comparing architectural tastes and debating camera angles, we enjoyed a "Brigadoon" morning as we and the town felt younger in the glow of our nostalgia.

We heard the strains of "Old Mill Stream" and "Daisy, Daisy" in four-part harmony coming from the ice-cream shop as we sailed along. "I can't resist the lure of chocolate ice cream and a barbershop quartet. It's got to be the ultimate in nostalgia," Joe said with a grin.

"We've already squandered our daily calorie limit on breakfast," I sighed.

"I'm sure all this pedaling will make up for the extra grams of fat and sugar," Joe insisted. "Not to mention all the hot kisses I expect to tempt you with today."

"Kisses don't burn up that many calories," I teased back.

"Mine will. You look adorable in that boater, and all this memory lane stuff is making me feel like a teenager again," he said, with a lecherous wriggle of his eyebrows.

I was only a tad flustered and breathless as we enjoyed a cone of double chocolate frozen sin and the first dozen or so of the promised kisses. After the ice cream had melted in our mouths and on our lips, the barbershop quartet, of course, sent us on our way to the tune of "Bicycle Built for Two."

For a moment, as we turned off Main Street, we thought the quartet had come along. Then we recognized the instrumental strains of the high school concert band just as we caught sight of them on the school lawn. The Gay Nineties pizzazz of boaters and red bow ties set off their usual black-and-white formality, and the midday sunshine cast the perfect backdrop for a cavalcade of American music, from pioneer folk tunes through jazz and blues and on to show tunes and popular standards with sidebars of American classical and rock. Joe and I circled the block a few dozen times absorbing the energy and renewing our own memories inextricably linked to the music.

"Do you think they'd play our song?" I asked. The

question was rhetorical. My Joe was far too practical to remember a melody neither of us had thought of in years.

"Shame on you for doubting the romance in my soul. Just proves how much we needed this date," he said with a put-upon look too blatant to be real. Leaning the bike against a tree, he dragged me up to the bandstand, whispered to the bandmaster, and whirled me off in a dance worthy of a candlelit ballroom. The band took a break, and, holding hands, we drifted back to our transportation.

Reluctantly, we aimed the bike toward the only hill in town. I needed an encouraging pat on the fanny and a kiss or two, but we made it to the top and the church strawberry festival awaiting us there. Over fresh lemonade and strawberry shortcake, we caught up with old friends, signed up for a moonlight river cruise in August, and snapped up the last two tickets for a hot air balloon ride outing the next weekend. We hadn't done that sort of thing in years, but the more things changed, the more they ought to, we reminded each other. Too soon, the refreshments and the afternoon ran out.

It was time to coast downhill toward the river and the picnic, family, and friends waiting for us. Chicken salad, ice cream cake, cold drinks, rides on the bike for the little ones, patriotic music from the bandstand, and a jubilant pink and gold sunset crowned the day. At full dark, magnificent readings of The Declaration of Independence, The Gettysburg Address, and Martin Luther King's "I Have A Dream" speech reminded us of what the holiday was all about. Back home in the cricket-chirping darkness, Joe and I shared a private waltz, a toast to our wonderfully nostalgic day and a new lifestyle, and—to get the kinks out, you understand—a shower built, like the bicycle, for two.

PATRICIA LEARY

❤ *Chef Tips* ❤

1. Add a Victorian touch to the day's apparel as mentioned with a white men's shirt, wide garters or large enough elastic bands, a straw boater from a costume shop, white pants. For the lady, culottes and a light puffy cotton or linen blouse, an old-fashioned bun, and a straw hat. Other Victorian touches as the weather permits.

2. If the traditional small town and entertainment are not available, a group could recreate this date and minimize the work and cost by dividing the day's program among them like a progressive dinner and ending with a potluck or take-out picnic at the local fireworks or concert. Recorded music can provide a variety of background ambiance. The amateur attempts at four-part harmony, square dancing, or similar additions should be amusing. Why not prizes for the winners or losers?

3. Have the lawn chairs, blanket, and picnic supper delivered by others.

Champagne Kisses

 Preparation
Time

Moderate

Cost

$$

Chef

Male

*Set a simple stage to pop the big question. A special
moment which you'll remember for a lifetime.*

Ingredients

Bottle of champagne (your favorite)

Crystal goblets

Fresh strawberries

One red rose

Silk blindfold

Engagement ring

I WHISTLED ALL THE WAY home from work.
Tonight, I thought, *I'll ask her tonight*. Miranda had
said seven o'clock would be fine. I checked my
watch and smiled, just two hours to go.

I turned the shower on and stepped in, adjusting the
spray. Hot needles rained down on my back. It felt good
to relax. I was keyed up. I can't blow it, I thought. She

was too perfect, the woman I had been unconsciously waiting for.

"Son of a—" I could have kicked myself. I'd forgotten to stop at the florist. Zipping my jeans, I swore again as I pulled on my boots. My friend Steve always said women need flowers. Would it make a difference . . . ?

"Jeez," I groaned, checking my watch. It would take me half an hour just to drive over to her apartment! I yanked the fridge open and grabbed the champagne and strawberries. Sprinting out to my Jeep, I threw it in reverse.

"Oh man—" I pulled up the emergency brake, "the glasses."

Once I had them, I got back in, reached for the stick shift, and looked over my shoulder to check for traffic. Mrs. Minick was waving, watering her roses . . . her roses!

I called out to her, waving, and couldn't help but grin. She was still trying to pay me for shoveling her out three months ago. "Going out, Tyler, dear?" she asked, a smile crinkling the softly weathered skin around her bright blue eyes.

"Yep," I said, smiling back.

"Miranda?"

"Right again, Mrs. Minick."

"She's such a nice girl," she paused. "Could make a man a good wife."

"I'm gonna ask her tonight!" I blurted out.

Mrs. Minick put a hand to her ample breast and gasped aloud, "Land sakes, Tyler Martin! You had better not be joking." Her eyes narrowed.

"No ma'am," I paused, "I'm late—"

She peered into the front seat of my car, "No flowers, young man?"

"I didn't have time—"

"You just wait right there," she said in a stern voice.

I watched her pull clippers out of her pocket and eye up her roses. She finally selected a single red rosebud. "Red," she said, blushing, "for your true love . . . it's more passionate, you know."

I got out of the car, hugged her close, and thanked her, "Wish me luck."

The dear woman beamed and nudged me back toward the car.

♥

"Where are we going?" Miranda asked for the third time, trying to remove the silk tie blindfold I'd placed across her eyes.

"Almost there," I said, not able to contain my grin.

I parked, then reached over and squeezed her hand. "I have to get something from the trunk. Please don't peek!" I pleaded.

She nodded. Lord, I love her, I thought as I got out of the car. It took me a couple of minutes before I could say, "OK . . . all set."

She grabbed at the blindfold and gasped, "Oh Tyler, the pier—"

"The first time I saw you," I said, suddenly all choked up.

"But—"

"Come on," I said, gently pulling her toward the bench

where I had set out two glasses filled to the brim with champagne and a dish of ripe, red strawberries.

"Miranda, why don't you sit here?"

"All right," she said slowly, suspicion clouding her amber eyes.

I took her hand in mine and raised it to my lips, "I love you, Randy," I said softly.

Her eyes misted over, "Oh, Ty—"

I handed her the rose and went down on one knee. "Miranda Daly, will you marry me?"

Silence . . . complete and utter silence. My entire body broke out into a cold sweat while she sat there just staring at me. The love of my life, my ideal woman, the perfect—

"Yes, Tyler, yes!" She pulled me up and wrapped herself around me.

I placed my hands on either side of her face and kissed her deeply. My woman, I thought, my wife.

A sense of peace spread through me as I held her close and breathed in the scent that was uniquely her own. Drawing away, I snagged a large berry and bit into one side of it, leaned toward her, and waited. She smiled and bit the other side. Our lips touched, the sweetness of the kiss rivaling that of the ripened berry.

"I love you, Tyler," she said softly.

"Thank the Lord!" I rasped, "because I love you, too."

I handed her a glass of champagne, let her sip it, and captured her lips again.

"Mmmm," she said drawing back, licking her lips.

Taking hold of her left hand, I slipped the heart-shaped diamond that had been burning a hole in my pocket onto her ring finger.

She smiled, eyes bright with unshed tears, "I could get used to champagne and your kisses."

I smiled and pulled her close. I had to kiss her again.

COLLEEN H. ADMIRAND

❤ *Chef Tips* ❤

1. Remember all the ingredients.
2. Bring a wrap in case the evening turns cool.
3. Most women want an engagement ring. Be prepared (not included in the cost).
4. Make sure you clean and package the strawberries properly.

Lost in Love

Preparation Time

Moderate

Cost

$$

Chef

Male

Winning the heart of your true love requires some effort, but the work is worthwhile in this unforgettable adventure.

Ingredients

Isolated outdoor place, preferably wilderness

Small plaque or professional quality sign with special message

Two glasses and bottle of celebratory vintage

*W*HEN I FOLLOWED Alan into the cave at the national park, I was excited. We both loved the outdoors and had been camping many times, but venturing into a glacial cave, even with other people, was a blue-ribbon thrill. I wasn't really nervous, though. We were with a small group of fellow wilderness fans, following a trained guide, hiking along well-worn paths. Besides, I felt safe anywhere with Alan.

As we entered the cave, I let my hand glide gently along

the wall, so smoothed from countless other adventurers. The guide's chatter about stalagmites and crystals hummed in the background. I felt so alive, so privileged, to be experiencing such natural splendors with the man of my dreams by my side.

As we hiked deeper into the cave, we needed our lanterns, but every time I looked back at Alan, his smile shone through the twilight. I knew I was in love and was loved back.

Eventually we came to an artificially lit, large cavernous room, with many passages leading away from it like arteries from a heart. People sipped their water and pointed out various formations.

"Come on, let's explore. This is boring," Alan whispered, and he gently pulled me away down one of the passages. Before I could protest about leaving the group, we were creeping down a narrow alley, and though the floor was smooth as if others had been here before, I was getting worried. This was not civilization, and as Alan twisted down into the darkness of the many tunnels leading off the path, I really began to worry.

"Alan, wait, we're going to get lost," I said, hearing my words echo back from the darkness ahead. Lost, lost, lost.

"Nah," Alan said, without breaking stride, "I think I can find my way back." He paused at the entrance to one dark portal before plunging in, then his warm hand grabbed my trembling one and pulled me after him.

"You *think* you can find—?" My heart pounded. We were lost. I knew it. Alan just wouldn't admit it. It figured. All this rugged outdoors man stuff made him too macho to own up to it, and now we were lost, never again to see the sunlight. Some day future explorers would find our bones crumbled together, like a scene from a Saturday matinee adventure movie: *Legend of the Lost Lovers.*

Shortly I could barely hear the voices of the other tourists, and then I couldn't hear them at all. I had no choice but to keep up with Alan, and eventually we came out into another large room. Even in my state of near panic, I gasped with delight. Our lanterns made the slippery wet walls sparkle like Ali Baba's hidden jewels. As Alan lifted high his lantern, I saw a plaque set into a small niche on one of the walls. What a relief! This was somewhere along the guided path. Eventually we would reach the others, or find our way out. My relief brought tears to my eyes, but when I walked around to read the plaque, I started crying for real.

Inscribed in elegant letters into the small brass plate was this poem:

> *The world abounds with vast, exciting sights,*
> *All magical when I have you by my side,*
> *But none would fill me with as much delight*
> *As those we'd share if you became my bride.*
> *Beloved, please say that you will marry me—*
> *Our most rewarding journey still is yet to be.*

There were two glasses and a bottle of champagne beside the plaque, and soon Alan was holding me in his arms.

My kiss was my answer. Suddenly lights went on and the rest of the tour group appeared, laughing and grinning. They had been in on the whole thing! Someone produced more glasses, and congratulations bounced off the walls, heartfelt wishes echoing from everywhere. "Listen," Alan whispered to me. "Mother Earth herself gives us her blessing."

LESLIE ROGALSKI

❤ *Chef Tips* ❤

1. This recipe can be adapted to any large park or secluded place of majesty. Even a stretch of beach would work. The fun is coming upon the plaque in the middle of nowhere, away from the civilized world. The Internet is great for tips on places to go in your region. Try a search in "National Parks" or "wilderness tours."

2. Have the plaque or sign printed and placed along with champagne and glasses in your selected spot ahead of time, enlisting the aid of local guides or rangers if necessary. If you can't get out to place the signs ahead of time, then ask the guide to help put them up during the "lights out" that is part of every cave tour. Make sure to swear your tour group to secrecy! If you have others touring with you, it's nice to have cups to share the bubbly.

3. Plastic champagne glasses are easier and safer, but nothing beats real crystal in a crystal cave.

One Small Step

Preparation Time

Long

Cost

$$

Chef

Male or Female

Humor can sometimes help us see what's really important.

Ingredients

Hand tools

Few pieces of wood

Saw

Nails, screws, hinges

Clever imagination

I REMEMBER the exact moment I fell in love with Sarah. We had just ordered two large skimmed cappuccinos at The Café Mocha when, bending down to pick up some change she had dropped, our heads collided. KABOOM!! At first, I couldn't decide if it was a mild concussion or her radiant smile, fiery red hair, and almost indescribably beautiful body that sent the rush of a dozen double expressos surging through my body.

"Here, let me get it," I offered, holding my head in pain.

♥

Monday morning coffee was a weekly ritual. About six of us would get together before work and commiserate about the previous weekend's social adventures. Sarah had recently joined the company and soon became part of the group. She was attractive, outgoing, and intelligent, so it wasn't long before I found myself drawn to her, and it didn't take a rocket scientist to see there was something happening between the two of us.

Both of us shared a love for the arts, the outdoors, and animals, and it seemed that whatever topic Sarah discussed, she projected such enthusiasm and passion that I couldn't help becoming caught up in it. Even the timing seemed just right; both of us had recently ended long-term relationships and were ready to move on. There was just one problem: our heights. Sarah was just a hair under 6' tall while I was barely 5'8". The height thing didn't bother me, but Sarah had apparently been so gangly as a child that it had become an almost pathological insecurity. While she never said it to me directly, it was clear that the only issue standing between our being friends and our being lovers was those damned four inches.

I wanted to be with her so much that it seemed as though Monday would never come. Finally, I mustered the courage to ask her out to dinner. Even though she agreed, I could still sense a certain hesitancy in her voice. That's when I realized that in order to overcome her hang-up, drastic action would be necessary.

Making use of some of the skills I had learned from my

high school shop teacher, "Eight Fingers" Moroney—a moniker downgraded from "Nine Fingers" after he accidentally cut off a pinkie while giving a freshman class lecture on shop safety, I took hammer, saw, nails, a few pieces of oak, and put together a quite acceptable example of a three-legged stool, making sure it was exactly four inches tall. I also hinged the legs and used a chisel to countersink them, so the final result when folded up was no larger than a notebook and not readily discernible as a stool. After a good stain and varnish, I attached a small brass inscription which read, "One small step for a man: one giant leap for love," and wrapped it with a bow on top.

I had made reservations at a very intimate downtown restaurant with romantic live music and arranged to have a certain song played on my cue. She was so stunning that evening, I had trouble swallowing my food. Finally, just before dessert, I handed her the package.

"What's this?"

"A present," I replied. "I thought it was something you could use . . . actually we could both use."

Sarah unwrapped the object, examined it, then read the inscription, still not realizing what it was. "I don't understand," she said, a bit perplexed.

"Here, I'll show you." I took it out of her hands. "But first, you'll have to stand up and close your eyes."

As she stood up, I cued the band, which began playing Gershwin's "Someone to Watch over You," then I unfolded the legs and stepped on the stool. We were now eye to eye as I put my hands on her cheeks and tenderly kissed her on the lips. Startled by the kiss, she opened her eyes and, seeing me at eye level, exclaimed, "Oh, my God . . . what are you doing . . . you're embarrassing me!"

"Embarrassing you?" I replied. "I'm the one standing on this stupid footstool."

She thought for a moment, then broke into a big grin."You're right, I've been a jerk. Come here, you silly." Pulling me close, she kissed me with such passion that I fell off the stool and we both landed on the floor, as some of the other diners laughed and applauded in support.

I rubbed my sore elbow before saying, "Thank God you don't wear high heels."

"How so?" she asked.

"There's no way I'm kissing you on stilts."

Her watery chuckle sounded in my ear. "I can't believe you actually went to all the trouble of making this just for me," she said. Then she smiled and whispered, "Maybe you're right. Maybe we can be more than just friends."

ROBERT S. COHEN

❤ *Chef Tips* ❤

1. Can be used for a variety of situations. Store-bought items are acceptable, but handmade really says you care.

2. Do it with a sense of fun in a nurturing surrounding. Remember you want her to laugh.

3. It's not for everyone. If he or she doesn't get it, you might have to reevaluate your own perceptions of what's really happening.

Wish on the Moon

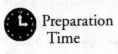 Preparation
Time

Long

 Cost

$$

Chef

Male or Female

*After 25 years of marriage, Julia and Sam can still
bring their New Year's Eve rendezvous and their
romance to a boil.*

Ingredients

Sparkling cider

Two crystal wineglasses

Seven vanilla candles

Herbie Mann CD

Floating candles for spa

Hanging pagoda with candle inside

One yellow rose

Spa and swimsuits

*I*N PREPARATION for our annual New Year's Eve
rendezvous, my husband, Sam, had carefully chilled
the cider and the wineglasses. The pagoda hung on a
pole, the candle within waiting for the flame to begin
the evening's festivities. The light would emanate from the

candle and reflect down on the Koi pond, close to the spa. Three vanilla-scented candles floated in the quiet spa, waiting to release their luminescence on the water's surface.

I worked late New Year's Eve and drove home on sparsely traveled roads. The moon crested over the ridge to the east, and I trembled with the anticipation of spending the evening with Sam. A full moon, a loving husband, peace, and quiet. I sighed with satisfaction. What more could one ask?

As I entered the house, the scent of vanilla washed over me. I looked up. Sam, clad only in black silk shorts, stood at the top of the stairs, holding a yellow rose, a provocative smile playing on his lips. As I ascended the stairs, Sam moved to meet me. He kissed me gently and handed me the flower, the back of his hand brushing my breast. I blushed like a schoolgirl. We walked up the stairs hand in hand, staring into each other's eyes. I heard the jazz of a favorite Herbie Mann CD playing and saw the soft glow from candles faintly flickering in the room.

Sam led me back to the bedroom where a solitary candle served as sentinel, barely illuminating the interior.

A beautiful green bathing suit was draped seductively over a chair. Letting go of my hand, Sam handed me the suit. He whispered, "I'd like to help you into this, but I will anticipate helping you out of it later." He grinned, kissed me again, and told me to meet him at the spa when I was ready, then left.

I floated from the house as if in a dream. Sam was already outside lighting the candles. The crisp, cold air sparkled with stars as the moon seemed to grow in the dark sky, its reflection dappling the waters of the spa and pond. The music, the candles, the rose. Even though the air was cold,

I felt no chill. Pausing on the back steps I looked up at the moon. It was full and ripe. Little ripples planed on the Koi pond as fish kissed the surface, then dove to safer depths.

I was overwhelmed with love for this man.

Sam waited by the spa as I walked toward him. The black silk shorts clung to his muscular thighs. He looked stunning at fifty-five. The gazebo around the spa was strung with small green twinkling lights and on the attached redwood bar stood a pillar candle, a bucket of ice holding the bottle of cider, and my antique Waterford crystal glasses. The combined light of the moon and candles danced like fire off the faceted goblets. We slipped into the spa, letting the cares of the world slide away, and watched the moon ascend higher and higher into the sky.

"Make a wish on the moon," Sam said.

"Do you remember the first time I met you?" I asked. "There was a full moon that night, and you said the same thing to me."

"And did that wish come true?"

I pondered a moment. "Most of it."

"'Most' meaning what?" Sam asked.

"I wished for world peace, a cure for cancer, healthy babies, and a sexy, good-looking, green-eyed man to share the rest of my life with."

"So make another wish," Sam said.

I hugged my mate hard and looked up at the moon. "I don't need any more wishes," I said. "This and you are more than I could have ever wished for."

"Then let's make a toast."

Sam poured the sparking cider into the wineglasses. He handed me one with a kiss and took the other himself.

"I want to toast you, Julia," Sam said, holding his glass

high. "You are the most beautiful, passionate, giving lover a man could ever know. You are the best of mothers. You held us together all those years I was struggling with the demon alcohol. Here's to sixteen years of my sobriety and sanity and your love and support."

Tears of joy streamed down my face. I held my glass to Sam's glass and heard the slightest clink from the crystal.

We drank our cider and placed our glasses back on the bar. Hugging him again, I gently traced his face with my fingers. Soft caresses over eyes, mouth, jawline. We kissed. A long kiss, full of promise and passion. We looked up at the moon.

Together we left the spa. Hand in hand, we strolled to the house, pausing briefly in the cold night to turn and look at the moon and share a kiss. "I love you so much, Julia."

"And I you, my dear sweet husband."

We entered the house then, locking the door and the world behind us.

LYN PALMER

❤ *Chef Tips* ❤

1. Be spontaneous—keep it simple and from the heart.
2. The cost rises if you find antique Waterford crystal wineglasses.
3. Take turns planning. Our celebrations just keep getting better and better, year to year. It's my turn next year to plan the anniversary of Sam's sobriety.
4. This recipe doesn't have to be followed exactly to get the desired results, but it doesn't hurt.

Catch of the Day

 Preparation Time

Long

 Cost

$$

 Chef

Male or Female

This date is ideal for the quirky, romantic soul who loves fun and informality.

Ingredients

Seafood meal

Wine & glasses

Beach props (as available—umbrella, towel, etc.)

Shells

Fishing game (homemade or borrowed)

Green-blue sheets

CD of sea sounds

Sand

RIGHT FROM THE TIME Andrea moved into the downstairs apartment, I thought she was something special—beautiful and happy. She bubbled with life and laughter. The first time she said hello and smiled at me something in my heart went "click." I wanted straight away to get to know her better, but it seemed I wasn't the only one captured by her. Although I tried hard over the next few months, I couldn't get through the crowd of admirers that surrounded her.

If only I could get her to notice me—lure her to my apartment somehow!

One day I was out on my balcony honing my tan when I overheard her telling a girlfriend, in her sweet husky drawl, that she missed home, missed the ocean, and missed being out with her friends—fishing.

Well, we might live in a landlocked city, but I got my perfect date idea right then.

First, I bought some shells and gift wrapped the prettiest one. Then I dug some sand from an empty yard and borrowed a set of green-blue sheets from a friend. It took me a while to track down a CD of sea sounds, but I found one in the local New Age health store. I also bought a stack of colored paper.

I spent most of Saturday buying what I needed and getting my apartment ready—I cut about fifty fish out of the paper and stuck paper clips on them, made a couple of rods out of sticks and string and magnets. I pushed the furniture back, spread the sea-colored cloth on the floor, sprinkled the sand around, and laid out the shells. I even put up a beach umbrella! I put some sparkling wine in the chiller and prepared dinner. I planned to have pan-fried fish (of course) with a lemon sauce, and I wanted everything to be ready to cook. Once I was organized, I knocked on Andrea's door.

When she opened it, my mouth dried out and my hands grew warm. She was so beautiful, I felt as if I'd been hit by a tidal wave. I asked her if she'd like to go fishing, and she tilted her head on one side to study me. A half-smile curved her beautiful, sensual mouth.

"Where?" she asked.

"I'll show you," I said.

"Tonight?" Her fine brows lifted and she studied me with her sea blue eyes.

"Best time for fishing," I said.

I was trying to be intriguing, and it must have worked because she smiled and said, "OK. Why not? Should I get my gear?"

"No, I've got everything," I said. "We'll have to go up to my apartment first." I could see she wasn't so certain about this, but she came with me, and I opened my apartment door and stood back to let her in.

The apartment "beach" looked great. The scene flowed out to the balcony and a single lamp glowed outside, sort of like the moon shining. The apartment was dark other than that, which added to the effect, and I had the New Age sea sounds playing softly.

She was silent for a minute and then she laughed. "Private beach, huh?" she asked, and glanced up at me, her eyes sparkling. "How much did you shell out for this?"

I grinned but didn't say anything. Good fishermen always keep their bait a secret.

I led Andrea to where I'd spread a blanket and cushions on the "beach" and offered her a fishing rod. By the time I showed her the "rock pool" and she saw the paper fish flapping in the breeze, she was laughing helplessly.

We had a wonderful time fishing on our own private beach, and later we cooked and ate the meal I'd prepared, pretending it was fish we'd just caught. When the real moon rose, we sat close together drinking wine that frothed like the surf, and I gave her my gift. She opened the silver-wrapped parcel slowly. Her eyes were suspiciously bright as she looked at me. I guess you could say that I'd caught her attention at last!

As she moved closer to me, I thought about that old saying—there were plenty of other fish in the sea. Well, maybe for some, but for me, Andrea was the best catch I'd ever have.

"Listen," she said, and held the shell to my ear. But all I could hear was the sound of my heart beating.

SUE EMMS

♥ *Chef Tips* ♥

1. Check to be sure that your date doesn't have a previous engagement before you make your preparations.

2. Bring in gourmet meals for a perfect touch, but remember it will cost more than stated above.

3. Spray your apartment with a sea-themed scent, e.g., Old Spice.

3.
RECIPES
THAT COST
LESS THAN
$120

Romance is love set on fire.

– Frank Cabiroy

Me, a Little Girl, and a Big Fish

 Preparation Time

Fast

 Cost

$$$

Chef

Male or Female

This recipe is designed to promote a deep bonding, and so, is intended only for those who are pursuing a long-term, full-time relationship with a single parent. It is guaranteed to get you lots of hugs.

Ingredients

Charter fishing boat (deep sea preferred)

Calm summer day

Dramamine

Sunscreen

Breakfast, fresh deli-made sandwiches, chips, soda

Cooler to hold the fish you catch

I'M IN LOVE with two girls! They're both pretty, intelligent, and charming. One of them loves to fish, the other one loves me. The woman I fell for is Ann. Her daughter, Ashley, was seven when we first met.

Although at first I was hesitant to pursue a relationship with Ann because I wasn't sure whether she really liked me or she wanted a father for Ashley, I decided it didn't matter. I knew in my heart that, in time, I could be that missing dad for Ashley and the love that Ann wanted in her life.

I watched for months in amazement as Ann kept up the dizzying pace of juggling a full-time job, motherhood, and a little time for us. I couldn't help but notice that all this didn't leave much time for Ann, the woman.

An idea came to me one day when I was driving Ann and Ashley back home from an outing at the bay. As we passed the pier, Ashley excitedly pointed out the people who were fishing and asked if we could stop and fish for a while. Not thinking, I laughed and told Ashley that I hated to fish. One look into the rearview mirror and I knew that I'd made a serious mistake. Her crestfallen face told me that she not only enjoyed fishing, but was hoping that she'd get some of my attention as well. Ann gave me a sympathetic smile, but I didn't feel any better. I dropped off my two subdued dates and headed home, openly chastising myself for missing the chance to know Ashley better. I didn't know exactly how, but I was going to remedy my thoughtlessness.

The next morning, I got up early and watched the weather station for the five-day forecast. No hurricanes, waterspouts, tornadoes, or other natural disasters on the horizon, so I decided that I'd take Ashley deep sea fishing on Saturday morning and Ann could have the morning to herself. Feeling slightly redeemed, I contacted Rudee's Inlet and got the number for a half-day charter. I arranged for Ashley and me to board the boat at 7:00 A.M. The plan was to fish for bass until noon and then return to the dock by one-thirty in the afternoon. I contacted the Tranquillity Spa and was assured there were appointments available for Saturday morning.

I rang Ann and told her what I wanted to do. She was speechless. She readily agreed and enthusiastically began to list all the things she'd do on "Pamper Ann" day.

"But I thought you hated fishing, Frank?" she asked just before I hung up.

"I don't hate it. I just don't like it much. But it'll make Ashley happy, and that's what I want to do."

Saturday morning, just as the sun was coming up over the horizon, I picked up Ashley and we stopped at the diner for a light breakfast. Then we stopped at the deli and ordered ham and cheese sandwiches, a six-pack of soda, and the biggest bag of chips we could find. Armed with our lunch and the new cooler we'd bought for all the fish we planned to catch, we headed for the inlet.

Want to lighten your heart? Watch a child have the time of her life. Not only did Ashley charm the early morning grumbles out of everyone on the boat, but up until almost quitting time, she'd caught the largest fish on the boat, making her first deep sea fishing trip the most memorable she'll probably ever have. By the time we docked, she no longer had the biggest fish, but we didn't care. Even the fact that I periodically had to visit the bathroom due to serious motion sickness didn't faze her. She fished with me; she fished without me. We ate lunch together, and then she fished some more. By the time we docked, we had some serious fish frying to do.

We picked up Ann and headed out to my place. Ashley and I cleaned our catch and got everything ready for our

Fish and Chips celebration, with Ashley regaling her mother, nonstop, about her adventures on the boat. Gory tales of chopping the squid, baiting her hook, and landing her own fish when the poor mate was too busy had her mother laughing until tears rolled down her face. When Ann looked up at me, she glowed. I knew it was more than the facial she'd gotten that morning at the spa.

As an exhausted Ashley slept on my sofa, Ann and I cleaned up the kitchen. When we'd put away the last of the dishes, she wrapped her arms around me and laid her head against my chest. I thought my heart would burst.

"Thank you so very much for today, Frank. It was a very sweet thing to do. Especially since I'm sure you paid dearly for being out on the rolling seas."

I kissed her silky hair and tightened my arms around her. "It was worth every single minute, Ann. I wouldn't trade today for a million dollars."

She tilted her head back and gave me a radiant smile. "And I wouldn't trade you for a million dollars."

FRANK CABIROY / NANCY QUATRANO

❤ *Chef Tips* ❤

1. Check the weather forecast, especially if you're prone to seasickness.

2. If you're feeling flush, hire a limousine for your "date's" mother's day of pampering.

Take Me Out to the Ball Game

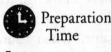 **Preparation Time**
Fast

Cost
$$$

Chef
Male or Female

Sometimes romance simmers in the learning stage,
before the anticipated date takes place.

Ingredients

Pair of baseball tickets
Bouquet of lilies
Motown music (or other favorite)
Hot dogs
Beer

I'M A DETECTIVE and make my living from uncovering information and following leads. Even so, I didn't need clues to tell me Laura was a woman I wanted to know better. One look at her coaching my niece's softball team put a lock on my interest. I gotta admit, I spent more time watching her than I did the game, but it's near impossible not to notice a leggy brunette in shorts and T-shirt jumping up and down, cheering every successful play.

Even more than her glossy brown hair and happy blue eyes, I liked her smile and the sound of her voice, warm and soft when she consoled a little girl who struck out. The first time I heard Laura laugh, my heart jumped as though it'd been hit with a 90-mile-an-hour fastball.

My niece introduced us after the game. When Laura shook my hand, I noticed the absence of an engagement or wedding ring on her finger. From then on I became a regular bleacher bum at the twice-weekly games. Pretty soon, I started helping out afterwards, gathering up the gear. Each time, Laura treated me warmly. And each time, I waved and yelled, "See ya," when she drove away.

After a couple weeks, I was no closer to a date than I had been at the start. All my life, I've never held back from asking a woman out. Then again, I didn't usually meet women like Laura. The season wouldn't last forever. A team of thugs with brass knuckles couldn't make me admit that I'd never asked because I was afraid she'd say no. What would a bright-eyed, soft-smiled grade school teacher like to do with a rough-around-the-edges guy with a crooked nose who spent much of his time alone tracking shadows?

It was time I found out. When I overheard Laura tell one of the team mothers she was heading to the market after the game, I got in my car and headed over there, making sure I arrived first. I could have followed her while she shopped. I do that for a living, and no subject ever spots me. But I wanted to romance Laura, not stalk her. So, about ten minutes after she arrived, I "arranged" to bump into her. She greeted me like an old friend, and in a matter of minutes, we were roaming the aisles together.

Most people don't realize how much of themselves they give away in the ordinary activities of daily life. All kinds of information come to light when you take time to look. Laura paused at the flower stand, studying the colorful blossoms. Her finger stroked a velvet rose idly, but when she spotted a container of bright stargazer lilies, her face broke out in a beaming smile as she leaned in to smell them. She quickly selected a few stalks of the crimson flowers and handed them to the vendor.

The butcher and she chatted like old friends about the Phillies' baseball chances for the year. Laura said she was looking forward to the upcoming series against the Dodgers.

From another booth, a boom box blared an old Smokey Robinson tune. Laura sang along, her voice flowing warm and smooth like brandy. I mentioned I'd heard a couple of the team mothers talking about a new restaurant and asked if she'd tried it yet.

"It's a little too fancy for my taste," she answered. "I think it's a waste of time to dress up and go someplace just to spend the night eating."

I fell a little harder for her. For me, food was a companion to fun, not the main attraction. And I tried to steer clear of places that demanded neckties.

Finally, our shopping excursion drew to an end. I carried some of Laura's bags to her car, ignoring the dryness in my throat. When she closed the trunk, I figured it was now or never.

"Listen, Laura, if you aren't doing anything Saturday, I have an extra ticket to the Phillies'-Dodgers' game at the Vet." I didn't, but figured I could score some without much trouble.

She looked surprised. "Mike, are you asking me for a date?"

Since she hadn't said "No thanks" right away, I figured I'd sweeten the deal. "I'll spring for dinner while we're there."

An eon passed while I waited. I needed an answer before I swallowed my tongue. "So, how 'bout it?"

"Beer and baseball? Sounds like my kind of a second date," she finally answered and, in that instant, my heart started beating again.

Then I realized what she'd said. "Second date? You mean our first."

Her smile shone with more wattage than a stadium full of lights. "Nah. This was our first date."

The days until Saturday dragged like a game in an endless rain delay. Driving over to pick Laura up, I figured I hadn't been this nervous since high school. Come to think of it, I must have been cooler back then. The sweet smell of stargazer lilies filled my car. Laura probably wouldn't want to tote the bouquet into the Vet, but I couldn't wait to see her smile when she saw them.

I'd popped a tape of Motown hits into the cassette player, and Marvin Gaye and Tammy Tyrell were singing a duet when I pulled up and saw Laura waiting on her front porch. Her eyes lit up when she saw me, and I hoped it wasn't only the prospect of seeing a game that made her happy.

On the ride to the stadium, we talked about the pitching matchups, my niece's improving batting average, and an insurance fraud case I was investigating. Laura tucked a single lily behind her ear. It should have looked silly underneath her baseball cap, but I thought it was the perfect touch. I sang backup while she imitated Diana Ross, and we were still laughing that I'd never make a Supreme when I parked the car.

My hand wasn't clammy at all when I linked it with Laura's while we walked into the Vet. Nowadays you can get all kinds of food at a game at inflated prices, but Laura was a traditionalist like me. We balanced beers and hot dogs that cost only slightly less than prime rib and good wine on our laps and settled in to our seats.

Now, I've always loved my sports, but I couldn't remember enjoying a game so much. Laura knew her baseball. I had almost as much fun watching her, loving the way she keyed in on the action. In the bottom of the ninth, when the Phils won the game on a pinch-hit homer, we jumped to our feet with the rest of the crowd. Laura threw her arms around me, surprising me with an exuberant kiss. I was sure the fireworks set off by the stadium crew actually exploded in my head.

Later on, we went for ice cream and talked for hours about our lives. After I dropped her off at home, her good night kiss stayed with me even after I finally stopped grinning. Laura had already agreed to a second, no, make that a third, date.

MARY STELLA

❤ *Chef Tips* ❤

1. Pay attention to what the object of your desire says or thinks.
2. Don't be afraid to take the chance.

Cruise to a Deserted Island

Preparation Time	Cost	Chef
Moderate	**$$$**	**Male or Female**

This is for the person who really wants to get to know her or his date, without any distractions.

Ingredients

Rented boat

Blanket

Cooler

Tropical style drinks

Picnic lunch (take-out)

Fresh pineapple for dessert

Paper cups and dishes

Fake flower lei

I FIRST MET RICH at a party hosted by a good friend. I found him easy to talk to and enjoyed listening to him. He seemed to have an endless fountain of interesting topics to expound upon. Unfortunately, I happened to be someone else's date that evening. When Rich sat down at a piano and played "Tara's Theme" from *Gone with the Wind*, my date paled in comparison.

At some point during the evening, I confessed that one of my fondest goals would be to go on a cruise to a tropical isle. A week later, I got a call from Rich.

"Would you like to go on a boat ride?" he asked.

Although it was late May, the weather had turned unseasonably warm and a boat ride sounded great, especially with a man as fascinating as Rich. I wore jeans and brought along a light jacket in case the weather turned cooler by the water. He picked me up and drove us to a marina where he rented a boat for the day, handing me the required emergency whistle.

"Use that if you get into trouble," the marina's owner instructed.

I looked at Rich and sensed that I could trust him. Besides, he worked with my good friend, who thought the world of him. Anyhow, the river was a busy place patrolled by the state police.

Rich helped me into the boat and then loaded in a cooler. Within minutes we were cruising out in the middle of the river. Allowing me to pilot the boat, he explained how to follow the channel markers. With his strong, warm hand covering mine as I held the throttle, I felt confident. A delightful tingle curled up my spine when his mouth lingered close to my ear, instructing me over the noise of the wind whipping past us. After a while, we reached an island in the middle of the river where the channel narrowed. The overgrown sandbar had a few scrawny trees for shade, some bayberry bushes, and marsh grass.

"Your tropical isle." He winked, reached into a storage box, and pulled out a flower lei. "Welcome to Paradise."

A laugh bubbled up in my throat as he placed the lei over my head. "That's silly. We're still in New Jersey."

"No, we aren't," he stated. "This is Starvation Island. "

Under his jeans he wore a bathing suit. As I watched him slip out of the jeans, I found myself appreciating his physique—maybe a little too much.

Then it occurred to me that he had anchored the boat in water that had to be at least four feet deep.

"I didn't bring a bathing suit." I worried.

"No problem." He smiled. Jumping out of the boat, he lifted up his arms. "Come on, I'll give you a ride."

I loved every minute of being held so tenderly. Then he went back to the boat to retrieve the blanket and the cooler. We had Piña Coladas (his specialty) along with some take-out Sweet and Sour Chicken.

Afterwards, we chatted while we strolled around our little island, picking up shells and beach glass. The time flew and soon we had to hurry to get the boat back to the marina. By then I knew Rich had all the qualities I like in a man.

I glanced about us before we left our little paradise and noticed the houses three hundred yards away on the shoreline, the state police boat whizzing by for at least the tenth time, and luxury cabin cruisers plying through the channel sedately. We had never been truly alone.

"Next time, could you find someplace a little less populated?" I questioned as he helped me back into the boat.

His eyes lit up with that devilish twinkle. "Your place, or mine?"

PENELOPE A. MARZEC

♥ *Chef Tips* ♥

1. Check out weather conditions beforehand.
2. It's better to rent a boat on a weekday—it's cheaper; there will be a lot less traffic on the water.

Relationship Repair

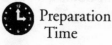

Preparation Time	Cost	Chef
Long	**$$$**	**Male**

*For the nonspontaneous fellow who wants
to push his envelope.*

Ingredients

Rickshaw	Violinist
Canoe in a pond	Rose petals
Pillow	Candles
Food	Picnic table
Picnic supplies	Bottled water
Grill	Plastic champagne glasses

S PARKS NEVER FLEW between us. Ours was a banked-fire passion, one that I expected to last a lifetime. That was why Beth's hostility blind-sided me the day she returned her engagement ring.

"The marriage is off!" she said.

"Sweetie, why are you upset?" I asked. "What did I do?"

"Don't 'Sweetie,' me. It's what you *didn't* do. You still live with your mother. You've never done anything spontaneous in your life. Everything has to fit into little boxes. I can't live with an accountant twenty-four hours a day."

"But I am an accountant," I said, confused. "And you've always loved me."

"Good-bye, George," she said, pushing me out the door.

I drove home slowly, trying to understand her anger. I'd always been amazed that she loved me, I a slight, prematurely balding, nearsighted man, she a bright, plump bird of a girl with flawless skin and carrot-colored hair. She'd always been gentle and kind, a natural kindergarten teacher.

We'd been engaged for three years. First, we waited until we'd saved enough for a down payment on a house. Then, Mother needed surgery, and she depended on me during her long recuperation. This morning, I'd asked Beth to wait six more months until I'd established a second office. Perhaps I shouldn't have done that. It was just that I wanted everything to be right for us. My parents had married when Dad was in school. They'd lived in student housing. It had always sounded messy and deprived.

Spontaneous. I went into the house and looked up "spontaneous" in the dictionary: "Acting in accordance with or resulting from a natural feeling, impulse, or tendency, without any constraint, effort, or premeditation." Beth was right. I never acted without planning. But for Beth, I could change. I would change. Impulses. I must have them, I thought.

I looked at the lifestyle section of the newspaper lying on the kitchen table. There was a picture of a local character, a grinning long-haired bearded man wearing spike heels and a short miniskirt and halter top. He posed beside his rickshaw, a homemade open carriage propelled by a bicycle. "Now that's spontaneous," I said aloud. "Maybe I can learn something from him."

A plan hadn't formed in my mind as I drove toward Sixth Street to find the rickshaw man. I deliberately let my thoughts wander. When I saw him, he was lounging in a lady's bathing suit, smoking a cigar, sitting on the red velvet rickshaw seat. "Do you give rides?" I asked him.

"To my friends," he answered.

"How about to a stranger and his girl for money."

"For $25 I'd rent the whole rig. You do your own pedaling."

"Done," I said.

"Cash," he said, "and you pay for damages."

I made arrangements to meet him later. I could take one of my nephews, I thought, to pedal the rickshaw. An hour later I'd gathered my nephews, Willie, Jim, and Carl, aged thirteen to seventeen. Showing them the newspaper picture, I explained my plan to be spontaneous.

"This is so great, Uncle George," Willie, the youngest, said.

"But you can't stop there. Just a ride isn't enough," Jim, the middle nephew, added.

"What else?" I asked.

"Roses," Willie said. "Girls love roses."

"But not just roses, rose petals raining over her," Carl said. "Listen, I'll pedal, and when we pass under something, the guys can drop rose petals."

"Yeah, yeah, the bridge," Willie said.

"And then we go to the lake. It's only four blocks. I can pedal that far," Carl said.

"We walk there all the time. She won't think that's spontaneous," I said.

"This time you rent a canoe," Jim said.

"OK," I agreed.

"I ought to play my violin," Willie said.

"In the canoe?" I asked.

"No, you need a dinner. You canoe to the point, tie up, and cook a steak on the grill. We can have it set up for you," Carl said.

"Then, I'll play," Willie said.

"I like it," I said.

"You can't stop there," Jim said.

"What else?"

"The Broken Spoke. It's close enough for the rickshaw. After dinner, you canoe back, I pedal you to the Spoke, and you go country western dancing."

"I don't know how," I said.

"I'll teach you," Jim said. "And I'll leave the car in the lot so you can drive home afterward."

Before I could back out, I called Beth. "Give me one last chance. We'll have a spontaneous date tonight."

"George, let's just have a clean break. I don't want to see you again."

"You have to go. I've already planned it."

"*Spontaneous* means *unplanned*," she said.

"I'll pick you up at seven. Dress casually." I hung up before she could refuse again.

After I towed the rickshaw to the house, I sprayed it with Lysol and covered the red velvet seat with one of Mother's quilts. Willie and I bought rose petals at the florist's and picnic supplies at the grocery store. The deli had prepared salad and dessert. Since the park didn't allow liquor, I bought bottled water and plastic champagne glasses.

Mother said, "You're crazy. Beth will never ride in that contraption, and you've let the boys talk you into all kinds of silliness."

At seven I arrived. When Beth saw the rickshaw, her jaw dropped. Spontaneously I bowed to her. "And there's more," I said.

The sun had turned the sky pink and orange as we passed under the bridge. Beth laughed as rose petals rained down on us, and cars honked for us. "There's more," I said.

At the lake our canoe was waiting, with a pillow for Beth to sit on. Ducks surrounded us as I paddled. A muskrat raised its head; turtles moved lazily along. Over the water the moon rose huge and bright. As we paddled up at the point, we saw that our fire was ready, the picnic table set complete with guttering candles. "There's more," I said.

I'd poured our water and served our steaks when Willie stepped from the shadows with his violin. He played his contest Vivaldi.

Beth's eyes had softened. She took my hand. "You can be spontaneous," she whispered.

"There's more," I said. The night went on. We canoed back. We rode in the rickshaw. We danced, joining the circle, kicking with the cowboys and their dates. Finally we sat in the swing on Beth's front porch.

"Is there more?" Beth asked.

"A whole lifetime, if you'll marry me as soon as possible," I said. I slipped the ring back on her finger.

She leaned up and kissed me. Spontaneously.

CAROLE DUNCAN BUCKMAN

❤ *Chef Tips* ❤

1. Find three creative nephews, or other support staff.
2. Check the weather report.
3. Use a CD player if you can't find a willing violinist.
4. Substitute ingredients with materials at hand.

The Fall(-ing in Love) Guy

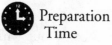 **Preparation Time**
Moderate

$ **Cost**
$$$

Chef
Male or Female

An ideal date for the extrovert who wants to declare his or her feelings in a fun, yet meaningful way.

Ingredients:

Tickets to a stage show

Large banner

I'M NOT CLUMSY BY NATURE but the first time I saw Angela in the building where I worked, I was so captivated by her slender physique, dark hair, and blue eyes that I didn't look where I was going and . . . yep, you got it. I tripped on the top step and landed on my knees at her feet. Well, I'm an amateur actor, so what could I do but make the most of my situation? I spread my arms wide and asked her to marry me.

She laughed. "I'm almost tempted," she said. "But I think you're a little short for me." She held out her hand to help me up and added, "Oh, that's better," as I got myself upright. Somewhere in the background a telephone burred and her grin widened. "Ah, the ring," she said. "Maybe this is meant to be after all."

Zing. Cupid's arrow hit its mark.

I introduced myself and asked her to come out with me, and after a bit of teasing, she agreed. We dated a lot over the next few weeks, going to the movies, dinner, dancing, even a ball game, and every date was better than the last. Angela bowled me over. She was intelligent, attractive, athletic, adventurous, and sexy. She looked great in whatever she wore, from business suits to blue jeans, and she tackled life head-on as if it were a gift, enjoyed everything from hot dogs to hula-hoops. When we were together, we laughed and talked and the time flew by. It got so I could hardly imagine a life without her.

One night we sat in the tiny garden of my little town house. We'd been playing monopoly, and she'd won by cheating outrageously; we'd laughed and argued then, but the evening had mellowed after a late supper. We sat with a bottle of red wine and talked until the moon set and the eastern horizon glowed with a crescent of pink. The mood was sweet, the air balmy, and we kissed in a way that melted me inside. I wanted to tell her that I was falling for her about as hard as a man could fall.

But I wanted to tell her in a way that was special and different and memorable and, sitting in the waning starlight, I got this great idea . . . .

All I had to do was track down a suitable venue and make arrangements with the management. Luckily they were enthusiastic about the idea, and we agreed on

Thursday night's show as being the ideal time. I phoned Angela and invited her out, but said nothing about my special arrangements.

Have you ever been in an airplane that has dropped suddenly and your stomach has swooped as if you were in free-fall? That's exactly what happened to me when I picked Angela up that night. She had her hair twisted in a knot, and she was stunning in a shimmering silver gown. She glowed, and I felt like the luckiest guy in the world.

The show was great, a romantic comedy that was perfect for the night. The actors sparkled and at the close of Act 3, they bowed to enthusiastic applause. The deep red velvet curtain fell slowly over the scene and a few seconds later, accompanied by a trumpet fanfare, another curtain fell over that.

This one was white, with big lettering on it.

Angela —
First I fell at your feet. Then I fell in love.
Now I want to fall into your arms. Forever.
Brad

Well, the audience started buzzing, but I watched Angela's face. Her lips moved as she read the words, and then shaped into a surprised "oh," and she darted a quick glance at me. Her expression told me she didn't know whether to laugh or cry. Next thing, a spotlight flared, and we were captured in a pool of light. The audience turned and applauded. I think they thought we were part of the show, but I wasn't acting about how I felt.

In the midst of the whistling and stomping, I leaned

close to Angela and said, "I feel as if the curtain's fallen on one part of my life and another show's about to open. I'd be honored if you'd be my star."

She laughed and wrapped her arms around my neck. "Oh, yes," she said, "but only if our First Act doesn't have an audience."

SUE EMMS

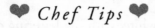

❤ *Chef Tips* ❤

1. Arrange for an usher to present your date with a bouquet of red roses.

2. For a touch of "star" quality, hire a limousine to take you home.

The Rose

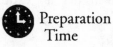

Preparation Time	Cost	Chef
Fast	**$$$**	**Female**

This date is for a woman who wants to take control of a budding relationship by showing what is sure to be seen as surprising initiative.

Ingredients

One long-stemmed rose

Plenty of money

$\mathcal{M}$Y ROOMMATE Todd and his girl-friend Cathy decided to set me up on a kind of blind date with her friend Karen. Cathy called me to tell me about Karen, since the two girls worked together in the university's admissions office, where people called them the "Siamese twins."

I'd showed up early at Cathy's place to find out a little about Karen before she arrived. The three of us had a drink while Cathy told me about Karen. "She's kind of a tomboy," Cathy said. "She's really cute. I think you'll like her."

I was only twenty-one, but I was already tired of "cute" girls and blind dates. Fortunately, Karen turned out to be 5'9" and cute wasn't it. Gorgeous was. Her Chinese mother and her Irish father had given her an exotic splendor. The possibilities intrigued me—an adventure instead of a blind date.

The four of us went dancing downtown at The Butcher Shop, a club that Cathy, Todd, and I went to all the time. Some guy both Todd and I knew from school came over to talk to us. He kept eyeing Karen, as if trying to get a feel for who her companion was. Before I could ask her to dance, he'd gotten Karen out onto the floor. For the rest of the night, it seemed, he played "keep away" with us.

After that night, I didn't think I'd ever hear from Karen again, and I hesitated to call her up and ask her out when I hadn't really put forth much effort to talk to her in person. So before leaving Cathy's place that night, I'd mentioned how beautiful I thought Karen was, and I figured that this information was sure to be passed on at work on Monday. If I had told Cathy that I was dying but not to mention a word except to Todd, rest assured on Monday morning I would be receiving a card signed by each member of her office, and Todd would still have no clue as to why.

Sure enough, Karen called me a couple of nights later to ask me out—a perfect way to find out we had similar feelings. I appreciate a woman who asks a man out; it really takes the pressure off him. She invited me to the Café Passé, a nightclub where she used to work. We agreed to meet there at 8:00 P.M. the following Saturday.

Saturday night, the club was packed. On the dance

floor, young people kicked and nodded like manic soccer stars. On the corner stage, a local band named Pleasure Latrine performed "The Rose of Tralee" on a tuba, an electric bass, and a snare drum loud enough to shatter steel. Not my favorite sports bar atmosphere, but then I had signed on for adventure.

I waited at the bar quite a while for Karen. Next to me sat a man who was breaking the filters off an entire pack of cigarettes, one at a time, while trying to explain to me how to catch a housefly barehanded. Not the kind of adventure I had in mind.

"Sorry I'm late," Karen said, kissing my cheek. "Here," she said, handing me a long-stemmed rose. "This is for you."

"I don't smoke," the man next to me said without looking at us.

Karen looked totally nonplussed, giving me hope. I placed the stem of the rose in my teeth and danced her backward a couple of feet to get away from him. I've never been fond of houseflies or barflies.

Karen waved hello to the woman working behind the bar, who brought my check over and started chatting.

A twenty-dollar bill folded like a butterfly materialized out of Karen's hand. It floated down onto the check; she slid it across the bar to her friend. "Let's get a table," she said, and winked at me. I took the rose in one hand and Karen by the other.

She led me through the noisy club, across the crowded dance floor, to a secluded table in the corner.

"Where's the rose?" she asked.

I held it up, but out of reach. I leaned close to her and

yelled over the music, "Too late to take it back! It's mine!"

At the table, Karen ordered two glasses of red wine from our waitress; she seemed to know her well, too. "You like red wine, don't you?" Karen asked me. "Cathy said you did."

"What else did she say about me?" I asked.

"She mentioned that you're ambidextrous," she said.

"That's not quite true," I said. "I'm switching back to left-handed."

"Back?" she asked.

"I was born left-handed," I said, "was brought up right-handed, and am now learning to do everything left-handed again. Writing, throwing, eating . . . ," I said, pretending to take a bite out of the rose.

"What else do you do left-handed?" she asked, raising her eyebrows.

"Lots of things," I said, smiling. "Just ask Todd."

"I don't want to hear about it," she said, holding her closed hand toward me. "No silly 'guy talk.' It's just you and me tonight."

As soon as the wine arrived, Karen reached behind my ear, like a magician, and produced a twenty, which she gave to the applauding waitress before I could even take my wallet out. I had the definite impression that tonight would be her treat. She certainly seemed like a scripted performer who would not take an argument regarding her show. Her style was okay with me.

"You know, I've never tried magic with either hand. Maybe you'd like to take on an apprentice?"

"Magic takes a lot of time. Maybe we should have dinner first?"

"Good call," I said. "Actually, I am kind of hungry."

"Great," she said, "Drink up. I'm taking you to dinner . . . somewhere quiet." She sipped her wine and blushed.

"Quiet is good," I said. I felt as if I were blushing, too.

Karen felt her cheeks and smiled. Then she touched mine. "It's from the wine," she said.

Outside the club, we held hands and walked down the street.

"There's a Cantonese restaurant I've been wanting to try," she said. "And no," she assured me, covering my mouth before I could speak, "I don't know anyone there. My mother told me that the food is wonderful. Of course, with my luck, she'll show up tonight."

"Don't you know how to make people disappear?" I asked.

She laughed. As we strolled, Karen kept leaning over, in front of and behind me, for all the world like a first grader keeping an eye on her only valentine. When I looked at her, she said, "Just making sure you still have the rose."

I asked her to stop and close her eyes.

"Tricks? You've been holding out on me?"

When she'd closed her eyes, I said, "Count to three." With each number I gently tapped her cheek with the rose, and at three I kissed her. We held the kiss for several moments, until Karen finally laughed and said, "Come on, I'm hungry."

The wind had picked up, so I put my arm around her.

"Does it bother you that I brought you a rose?" she asked me.

"No," I said, smiling. "Not at all."

"Cathy said you'd never go for it," Karen said.

"Well, she was wrong," I said. "I love beautiful things. Besides, every time I see a rose I'll think of that adorable blush when you drink red wine." Karen closed her eyes again and smiled.

"Anyway," I said, "no more 'girl talk.'" I leaned close and kissed her again. "I'm hungry."

JAMES MITCHELL

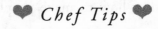

♥ *Chef Tips* ♥

1. Leave the rose unwrapped.
2. Have complete confidence in your plans.
3. Additional magic tricks are welcome.

Half a Ring

 Preparation Time	🪙 Cost	👨‍🍳 Chef
Fast	**$$$**	**Male**

This is the most romantic place in the world for a proposal, especially if you are an outdoor type.

Ingredients

Picnic basket with your favorite picnic
Blanket
Bottle of champagne
Champagne flutes
Single white rose
Road map

"**W**HERE are we going?" I asked again. "You'll see." Jack's mysterious smile warned me not to question further. He is a master secret keeper.

Wonder what he has in mind? We were heading north, into the mountains. Too late in the day to enjoy the last of the fall colors. Too warm, even now in mid-November, to hope for snow at higher elevations. I leaned back against the seat and sighed, "Well, I am a visual learner. Okay, I'll see."

I looked past him toward the setting sun. The sky slipped from lemon to crimson behind the trees atop the farthest ridge. Silhouetted against the last light, the bare limbs looked like black lace. I studied the effect, trying to decide how I would describe the scene in the book I'm always writing in my head. Suddenly Jack pointed across me, toward my window. A full moon had just cleared the sharp escarpment to the east.

"Oh, this is too good." I laughed. "How long have you been planning this adventure?"

"Since the first day I met you."

Something in his voice made me look at him then. His red hair looked dark auburn in the failing light, and the freckles that gave him his perpetually boyish look were invisible. I could see the determined jut to his chin.

Oh, boy, this is not just another one of our inexpensive dates. Something's up.

Jack and I met while we were both in graduate school. Like most grad students, we lived in not-so-genteel poverty, not minding too much because we counted it an investment toward the future, and besides, all of our friends were in similar circumstances. Much of our time together had been spent studying side by side in the library or watching rented movies. A real splurge could mean a red rose in a bud vase on a picnic blanket in the country.

I glanced into the back seat, and there was the familiar

basket, covered with the veteran red plaid blanket. "What's for dinner?" I tried to sound casual.

"The usual. Bread and cheese. A thermos of coffee." Even though it was too dark to see them by now, I knew his eyes were twinkling. One thousand, two thousand, a comedian's timing. "And champagne."

That jerked my head around. Champagne? On *his* budget? I threw him a look along my shoulder, then turned and stared at the moon, my thoughts racing. We rode in silence until a state park sign loomed beside the road.

"Do you know about this place?" At last, he had started a conversation.

"Only that it's here."

"Good." He wheeled into the parking lot.

I was surprised to see other cars there. Campers? But I saw no signs of tents or tables.

Jack lifted the picnic basket from the back seat and grabbed our jackets. He took my hand and set off on a footpath that was marked with a sign I couldn't read, even in the moonlight. I could hear rushing water away in the distance. We walked toward the sound.

My eyes grew accustomed to the darkness, and the moon rose higher, turning the surrounding woods into shadows pierced by shafts of light. The water's roar grew deafening, and I realized we must be heading straight for the falls.

I felt Jack's hand in the middle of my back, giving me a familiar nudge of encouragement up the last steep incline. And then we were there.

The waterfall itself was breathtaking, taller than a six-story building and twice as wide as it was tall. The water fell like a white wall, crashing onto boulders at its base, sending up a cloud of fine mist that hung in the air.

Then I saw what Jack had brought me here to see. I gasped, then let out the air in a long, "O-o-oh, my!"

Jack, standing behind me, set the picnic basket down and gently put his arms around my shoulders, drawing me toward him. "Incredible, isn't it?" he breathed against my ear.

The light of the full moon caught in the prism of the mist and shattered into its component colors, creating a "moonbow" that arched across the falls. Its pastel loveliness against the width of the creaming water was like seeing a reflection in pewter.

We stood, awestruck and silent, for a long while, drinking in the magical beauty of the place. Gradually, I became aware that there were other people standing in the shadows—a couple, like us, standing close, and off to one side, a family with young children. Even the kids were quiet, staring at the scene before them.

At last, Jack stirred and stooped to retrieve something from the basket. He stood again and, still behind me, wrapped his arms around me. In his hand gleamed a single white rose, its ivory petals perfect in this landscape of pearl and silver.

He turned me, by my shoulders, until I was facing him. The lambent light lay across his freckles, but his eyes were dark.

"I can't give you a ring, but if you will accept half a ring—a moonbow—and a rose as my pledge, I promise you, someday . . . ."

I kissed him then, and his lips tasted of mist and moonlight and the promise of forever.

LYNN WHITED HUTTON

💜 *Chef Tips* 💜

1. Cost depends on how far away you are from a "moonbow," whether the trip will involve an overnight stay, and how expensive your champagne is.

2. Be sure you know the date of the next full moon.

3. Make sure the weather will be clear, so the full moon makes the "moonbow."

4. Driving time to Cumberland Falls State Park (twenty miles southwest of Corbin, KY, on SR 90) varies.

5. Put the rose in a tube with water, so it will keep for the drive.

A Knight to Remember

 Preparation Time

Long

 Cost

$$$

 Chef

Male or Female

This is a date that is meant to impress someone special. It is guaranteed to demonstrate passion, creativity, and effort.

Ingredients:

Poster board

Two dozen candles

Baroque music

Page costume

Medieval princess costume

Index cards

Magic markers

Three courses of authentic medieval foods

Optional ingredients:

Plastic knight armor

Toy swords

Additional medieval garb

Mannequins

I DON'T THINK that I will ever forget the night that I met Priscilla. It was a Sunday night in November, and I was looking for some interesting reading material at a local bookstore. She was seated in the inspirational book section, completely immersed in what she was reading. I, on the other hand, was immobilized in the self-help section trying to muster up the courage to introduce myself to her.

I walked over to her and said, "Excuse me, are you finding everything all right?"

She looked up, smiled, and replied, "Yes, thank you."

I nodded and said, "Good, because even though I don't work here, I would hate for you to be disappointed." She must have thought I was insane. But it made her laugh, and we had a wonderful conversation and agreed to get together again.

The following week we went to dinner, and it was as though we had known each other for our entire lives. Our time together was magical. We began to date regularly. As we approached the beginning of our third month of dating, I decided to do something exceptional to show her that she was very special to me.

In one of our many telephone conversations, she'd mentioned that she loved castles. As I hung up the phone, I devised a wonderful date. I would create a moment from her favorite time period: The Middle Ages.

I told her, a week in advance, that I wanted to cook her a special dinner at my home. What I didn't tell her was that it would be much more than a dinner. I decided to turn my home into the fantasy castle that she had described in one of our earliest conversations.

On Monday, I bought ten sheets of poster board and cut out bricks for the top of my mock castle. I attached the bricks to every wall in my home. I created a banner that said "Ye Olde Tavern."

On Tuesday, I went to a local costume rental place, explained to the owner what I was doing, and told him that I wanted to rent two costumes, which would be worn.

I also asked him if I could get a discount on costumes that would be used for decorations. He agreed, and for a little over one hundred dollars I rented the following items: a page costume (for me to wear), a princess costume (for her to wear), a mannequin, a dragon mask, a horse mask, several plastic swords, and plastic knight armor.

On Wednesday, I constructed a knight on a horse out of pillows, sheets, the mannequin, and the plastic armor. I placed it in one corner of my living room. Then I mounted the dragon on a piece of wood and placed it on an adjacent wall. I placed the crossed swords on another wall and set candleholders all over my home.

On Thursday, I purchased two dozen candles and placed them in the candleholders. I created index cards with cute little sayings on them and placed them throughout my home. The sayings were things like "Page me," "Joust you and me," and "I hope that this knight does not drag-on."

Friday was the day of our date. I left work early that day, so that I could go home and make final preparations. I wanted things to be as authentic as possible, so I did some research about medieval feasts. I discovered that people ate many courses, beginning with something light and progressing to more filling foods with each course. With that information in mind, I prepared the following menu:

Course 1 — Chicken broth with sliced vegetables.
Course 2 — A small salad.
Course 3 — Cornish game hens that had been
                 marinated in wine and cooked over an
                 open flame.

While I was cooking them, I anticipated how much fun it would be to eat with our fingers placing morsels of food into each other's mouths. I planned to serve apple cider in large gold goblets. For dessert I wanted something rich and sweet, so I made a spice cake full of nuts and raisins.

Fifteen minutes before she was scheduled to arrive, I got out my baroque CDs and turned on the stereo. The music and candlelight created a nice atmosphere. I got dressed in my page costume and attached my sign to the front door.

I heard her car pull into my driveway and went outside to meet her. When she saw how I was dressed, she laughed. My neighbors laughed too. I opened her car door and kissed her hand and said, "Milady, I am here to serf you." She smiled and allowed me to escort her.

I led her into my home, and she was astonished at what I had created. She walked around the house reading my notes and laughing. When the laughter subsided, I touched her hand and gently kissed her on the cheek. As I put my arms around her, I whispered into her ear, "You mean so very much to me." I saw her eyes fill and knew that she felt cherished. We embraced for a few moments, and then I led her to a closet and took out her costume— a beautiful purple satin gown with a matching headpiece and pearls for buttons.

She was pleased that I'd picked out a costume exactly her size. The note I'd attached to the dress said, "To Priscilla, my damsel, who I hope will fit into dis-dress."

She went into the bathroom and changed into the gown. I could hear her soft laughter. By the time she emerged from the room, I knew that I had found my princess. We spent the rest of the evening laughing, feasting, and enjoying our special moment in time.

MICHAEL MATTEO

♥ *Chef Tips* ♥

1. The medieval theme is just a suggestion. The key to my date being so wonderful was that she appreciated my taking something that she mentioned in passing and made it happen.

2. The same kind of date could be accomplished with any of the following themes—just be creative!

3. Potential Themes: Oriental, Egyptian, 1920s, Roman, Country Western, etc.

4. Suggested books on medieval foods:
   - *Fabulous Feasts: Medieval Cookery and Ceremony* by Madeleine Cosman.
   - *The Art of Cookery in the Middle Ages* by Terrence Scully.

4.
Recipes
that Cost
less than
$160

The romantics are the adventurers.

– Frank Cabiroy

Scrumptious Saturday

 Preparation
Time

Moderate

Cost

$$$$

Chef

Female

This evening is specifically designed to take good care of your partner and, in turn, the "chef" as well. Ideal to put some of the romance back into a relationship that suffers from the effects of the "same ole" syndrome.

Ingredients:

Hotel/motel
room

Nightwear —
easily removable

Scented candles

Scented bath oil

Bottle of wine

Corkscrew

Wine glasses

Picnic for two

Music

Invitation

I LOVE MY HUSBAND, very much. He's tall, dark, handsome and he works hard to take good care of us. So, like most people who get caught up in the everyday things like kids, jobs, carpools, shopping, home repairs and the like, we somehow never have much time for each other.

One day when I came into the house from running errands, I found a red rose on the table. No note, no husband, just the rose. The kids tore past me and slashed through the living room like the tornadoes that they are, and I immediately clicked into my best Gestapo routine in an effort to salvage the furniture. Hubby walked in to total chaos, and it was almost three hours before I got to thank him for the rose and the loving thoughts behind it. He was less than placated with my hug and kiss. It was then that I realized that this good man was feeling like he'd taken last place in my life. I decided that I'd have to come up with some way to let him know that, even though he *seems* to come last on my list of urgent priorities, he's really at the top!

I threw the kids outside for the afternoon and poured a cup of tea. I studied the all-too-crowded calendar and picked a Saturday that looked free of obligatory chores, meetings, and work obligations. I called my in-laws. They agreed to take the kids for the weekend, so I could drop them off on Friday and pick them up on Sunday. Knowing how much my man loves the sea, I called some of the hotels and motels listed along the shore, from Belmar to Seaside Park. I found one that boasted cozy rooms complete with large tubs, small fireplaces, and reasonable rates. I booked the room for the Saturday that I chose and dashed downstairs to the computer. I designed an invitation to my husband, requesting that he meet me for dinner at the hotel I had chosen, at seven o'clock, explaining that I had a special meeting late that afternoon, but with the kids away, I wanted to treat him to an ocean-side dinner. (Black tie was optional.)

I love to hear my man laugh. Sadly, we don't spend enough time laughing with each other. I thought it would be fun to put a picnic together of foods we would enjoy feeding each other. These included bananas, fresh peaches, seedless grapes, a variety of cheeses, a fresh baked loaf of French bread, and a bottle of his favorite California Merlot. I happened to have my mother's old wicker picnic basket, which held everything beautifully. I topped it off with brownies from the gourmet bakery, two crystal wine goblets, and two cans of whipped cream, just to be daring. I had the greatest time, imagining what fun we could have in that room.

I packed a bag with clean clothes for both of us, a slinky nighty I hadn't worn in years, two candles, and scented bath oil. I grabbed the portable CD player, two of hubby's favorite jazz albums, and stowed the food along with everything else in the back seat of my car. Knowing I had to be on the road before he came home from work, I left the invitation taped to the kitchen door and headed for the hotel, so I would be there ahead of him in time to have the room ready.

By six-forty, I had the bath run, the candles lit, the wine on ice, and a small fire going in the fireplace. I spread the contents of our picnic beside the beautiful porcelain tub and changed into my nighty, knowing that my very prompt husband would be arriving shortly. Because there was no restaurant at this hotel, I knew he'd have to go into the lobby and ask for help. I left word and a nice tip with the receptionist to send him to our room. I put on one of his favorite CDs and settled down on the bed to wait for my hero.

His gentle knock on the door told me that he was on to my surprise. I opened it for him, stretching up on my toes to wrap my arms around him. "I love you, very much," I whispered just before I kissed him in the firelight.

"I love you, too," he answered when he finally pulled away. He removed his jacket and looked around. As he slipped out of his loafers, he pulled me to his chest. In the candlelight it was easy to get lost in his deep, dark eyes. "This is too perfect. I'd never imagine anything like this, from you."

I smiled at him and handed him a glass of wine. "I know. That's what made it all fun. Now, come over here and let me get you comfortable. Tonight, I'm gonna show you just how special you are to me." I began to unbutton his lightly starched shirt. He wrapped his arms around me, stilling my busy fingers.

"And I," he whispered, as he pulled me down on the floor by the fireplace, "am going to love each and every moment."

Nancy Quatrano

♥ Chef Tips ♥

1. Doing this at home doesn't work.
2. Your hotel/motel does not have to be expensive, but cozy is important. No high traffic areas.
3. Double check the calendar to make sure everyone is available.
4. Be sure to use scents that your partner likes (candles, bath oils, whipped cream?).

Ham and Rye on a Harley

 Preparation
Time

Moderate

 Cost

$$$$

 Chef

Female

---

*This date is not for the faint of heart. For those
willing to risk it, the rewards are abundant.*

Ingredients

Deli food

Homemade apple pie

Blanket

Imported ale

Frosted mugs

Paper plates

Portable CD player

Napkins

Utensils

Harley (bright and
shiny)

*A*FEW YEARS AGO I started thinking about Jim again—a familiar
memory, conjuring up old feelings,
and triggered by certain songs, those 60s bikers hits in
particular. So, when his phone call came out of the blue
one sunny morning last summer, I was truly surprised. It
was almost as though he was reading my mind, picking

up the dust of memories left huddled in the corners of my soul. Suddenly thirty years melted away, and we were teenagers again, anxious and hopeful.

We had dated in high school, drawn together by our differences. Jim was the cool older kid in the black leather jacket, I the shy, brooding 16-year-old trying to fit in, both thinking no one understood us.

His motorcycle was what attracted me first, a lovely mass of silver and black metal, and him sitting astride its chassis, the smooth curves of the jacket wrapped round him like ribbon on a present.

We "went together" all summer, our diverse lives entwined like love knots tied to string. We spent the warm, desperate nights riding double on the bike, ending up under the cool, damp hollow of the railroad trestle, snuggled against the world, dancing to the music from our portable radio. That impassioned season ended when Jim left for the Navy.

As our discussion continued, I vowed that this time would be different. I wouldn't shy away, wouldn't lose him to some silly Presbyterian ethic. So when the conversation stalled, empty as an awaiting tomb, I blurted out, "Let's meet for dinner. A week from today. I'll make all the arrangements. Pick you up at seven."

Now, I had to come up with a unique approach to this long-awaited date. It had to be perfect, a subtle blend of yesterday, melding old feelings with today's lifestyle. First, I went to the attic and searched through a box of old clothes I'd been carrying with me from place to place over the years, sure that I'd need them someday. And there, crowded among musty books and used furniture,

I found the black denim jeans with little zippers at the ankles, faded to just the right patina, and the cashmere twin set, still smelling of Chantilly.

This gave me the idea I needed to plan the perfect night. I started with the Yellow Pages, looking up anywhere in the vicinity that rented Harley Davidsons—found Dino's Bike Shop on the second try. He had the exact cycle I needed, a Harley all polished and shiny like I remembered, just waiting for me. When Saturday came, I met with Dino for a few instructions and a practice run. He even threw in the leather jackets and helmets.

I had just enough time to pick up the prosciutto, hot mustard, and potato salad from the Gourmet Deli, then on to the bakery for fresh rye bread. I'd baked the apple pie myself earlier that morning, not trusting anyone's recipe but my mother's, one I hoped Jim would remember.

I'd also had a six-pack of imported ale cooling all day, wrapped securely now in the side compartment of the bike. Red and white checkered napkins held all the necessary accessories, and I felt like that young girl again, carefree, with the warm July air blowing through my hair.

"Whoa, Baby," slipped almost like a whistle from his lips when I picked Jim up, astonishment crossing his face. The years had been good to him, his middle age giving off a sense of virility, like a panther on the prowl. I could tell he was pleased with me, too. The same wink of approval gleaned so long ago quickly washed over his right eye.

"Can you really handle that thing?" Jim wanted to know, hesitation growing into a faint, slow smile that clung like an edge of light to his lips.

I stomped down hard on the accelerator and let the bike guide me smoothly around the corner. I pulled up to him again with a quiet certainty, very pleased with myself, somewhat like a boa constrictor that's just enjoyed a satisfying lunch, and threw my head back haughtily.

"Hop on, Slick," I said glibly, drunk on my own high spirits. As I tossed him the extra jacket and helmet, I grinned, not yet wanting to answer his question, "Where are we going?"

Our bodies seemed to blend perfectly again, riding double in the summer heat that dropped from the sky like a blanket of steam. I approached the old trestle, furtive and slow as if denying a hidden sin, found a smooth spot to spread out the blanket, and readied the meal—deftly cutting the bread, piling up the prosciutto, spooning out potato salad. We clinked the chilled mugs of ale as if toasting with expensive champagne, but enjoyed its heady bite much more.

As we finished up the meal, the sultry night sky changed from pink salmon to mother-of-pearl, then washed in night black rimmed in silver. Somewhere in the distance, crickets chirped in harmony with the music coming from the portable disc player. As we laughed and talked, old passion ignited.

"Remember our song?" Jim asked. "We used to push every button on the radio until we heard it, then start all over again."

"Unchained Melody," I responded, and in unison we started humming lyrics that pierced our minds in bolts, like flashes of lightning.

And just as the half moon sailed like a moth up the midnight sky, Jim asked me to dance. It was the two of us again, joined like two roots twining into a single flower.

That night we learned that the love of the older and more disciplined heart burns like gray coals, deep and inextinguishable.

SHARON L. KONSCHAK

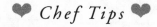

❤ *Chef Tips* ❤

1. Pack mugs carefully in Styrofoam holders to keep them cold.
2. Check batteries for CD player.
3. Enjoy.

The Business of Love

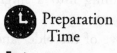 Preparation Time
Fast

💰 Cost
$$$$

👨‍🍳 Chef
Male or Female

For the couple that cares . . .

Ingredients

Stack of your own business cards

5" x 7" note card

Flowers

Hotel room

RAPPED IN LOVE and the scent of orange blossoms, Steve and I got married four years ago. I think we love each other more now than we did then but somehow, things have become a little . . . humdrum. At least, that's what I feel. Mornings are always a rush to get to work, our days are busy and our nights—well, our nights are uneventful.

I lay in bed last night, listening to my husband and lover breathing and wondered when it was we'd started taking each other for granted. When it was that the magic had dimmed? How was it we stayed in bed more because we were tired, rather than hungry to hold each other?

Moonlight pattered through our open window, and I rolled over to study Steve's sleep-shadowed face. He's so handsome, so strong, and my heart melted with love for him. I thought, he deserves better than this and so do I.

Our anniversary fell the next week, and I got a wonderful idea for celebrating it. I knew just how to put the magic, the spice, back into our marriage.

I took a pile of Steve's business cards with me to work and, during my lunchtime, wrote them up. Sweet nothings, for his eyes only. All the things that made me shiver to my soul, I wrote them out. I love the way you sing in the shower. I love the way you always lose your car keys. I love your sexy touch. I love the way you say "Hi," when you answer the phone. I love that you care about little birds that fall out of their nests and that you'll climb the tree to put them back. All those things, big and little, that made me fall in love with him in the first place, I wrote them out. I wrote one last special message on a giant-sized business card I made out of a 5" x 7" note card.

Then I made two very important bookings for the big day.

On our anniversary, I told Steve I had something important to do at work and left early. Before I left, I tucked one of my cards into his pants pockets, another into his jacket, his briefcase, under the windshield wiper of his car, on the front seat. Then I raced to his office and hid some in his desk, pinned one on his wall, left one addressed to him in an envelope on his secretary's desk, another with his receptionist. After that I headed down to his favorite lunch bar and left a couple more cards, in envelopes, for him there. Manny, the proprietor, was a bit of a card himself and happy to help out.

Just to add to the intrigue, I wouldn't take any of Steve's phone calls during the day. After lunch, I took a break and put fresh cards on and in his car, and, most importantly, left the address of where we were to meet for dinner.

I went home and freshened up, made it back to A Taste of Italy, our restaurant, with minutes to spare. Steve arrived in a rush, with a big armful of roses, his eyes alight with love, and that wonderful mouth of his curved in a grin. He bent and kissed me, and my stomach turned somersaults. "Happy Anniversary," I said.

He said, "I'd forgotten, you know."

I knew, but that was OK. He'd remembered now. How couldn't he, when here we sat in the restaurant where we'd had our very first date? We drank the same wine as we had that night and ordered the same meals. Steve dealt out the cards, telling me where he'd found them and what they meant to him. We were both emotional and giggly by the end of the first course. He'd remembered now. How couldn't he, when here we were in our very special restaurant where we'd shared, not just our first date, but also a special meal, right before we'd spent our first night together? Except that this time, I'd booked the room ahead and done a little on-site preparation.

Snuggled together, we walked to the nearby Hotel Armitage and made our way up to our room. Steve swung me up in his arms and carried me to the bed—there, lying on the cover was my last, special card. Surrounded by little red hearts and flowers, the words said, "For Always."

"You bet," said Steve huskily, and when he lay me on the bed and looked deep in my eyes, I knew the magic was back.

SUE EMMS

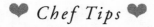

Chef Tips

1. Any kind of card or notepaper will do, of course.
2. Re-creating any early lovely, shared moment tends to call up those early special emotions, but each time around makes them deeper.

Cinderella

 Preparation Time
Long

 Cost
$$$$

 Chef
Male

Unique way of making someone feel special, with a day-after reminder.

Ingredients

Limousine

Violinist

Messenger

Day-after gift based upon the evening's conversation

"WINNIE THE POOH, Winnie the Pooh" trilled merrily from the girls' room, as I picked up a paring knife and spread a newspaper on the kitchen table. I hadn't read it, but it didn't matter. My officemate, Melissa, had ducked out of the office early for a dinner date, adding two hours of unpaid overtime to my already exhausting day. By the time I gave Meredith and Kacie dinner, helped them with their homework, and supervised their baths, the day would be fifteen hours old, and I'd be too tired to read anything heavier than "Cinderella" for them.

The paper fell open to the singles ads. No sense in reading those. As soon as a guy hears a woman has two kids, he goes screaming off the battlements into the moat. Singles ads: same old, same old.

But one was cute—I'm the One Guy to Have When You're Having Only One. A takeoff on the old beer commercial, but clever—and somehow sincere. What if he meant it? What if—? No, he couldn't be looking for someone who had to be up before dawn to clean the house, do laundry, get the kids off to school, and get herself off to work. Someone who couldn't afford an extra pair of panty hose, let alone a glamorous dating wardrobe. Someone with a drudge job at the bottom of the office food chain. No, the ad was of no use to me except for the disposing of potato peelings.

I followed my own advice and tossed the soggy lump into the trash and put the potatoes on to boil while the meatloaf baked. The rest of the evening would be another whirlwind of homework, baths, and story time.

"Cinderellie, Cinderellie," the music called.

"Right here on duty," I muttered, "with no fairy godmother waiting in the wings." I took a deep breath. "Still, I've got two magic mice, and—even tired, lonely, and broke—I wouldn't trade them in for anything."

The next day I couldn't believe the traffic. Figured I'd get fired for sure. *Please God, give me a break. I need every dollar*, I thought, making a mad dash down the hall and into the office.

"Well, it's about time you got in! These reports have to

be processed immediately," Cindy, another co-worker, barked, "and you didn't finish yesterday's work before you left." She nudged Melissa and said, "Hey, you'll never guess where Frank's taking me for Valentine's Day!" Another day—same old, same old.

That night, another batch of potatoes. I'd been staring at this guy's ads in the paper every night for weeks; there were seven of them now. He'd become a celebrity. There was even an article about him. Great job, volunteer work with kids, looked like a regular guy—yet sexy. No wonder one woman wrote him a song, and another offered to show up wearing only a raincoat. How could I compete with that? What could I possibly say if I answered his ads? Well, what difference did it make? The worst he could say was no. Besides everybody ought to meet a guy like that once in her life. Nothing ventured, nothing gained. I'd give it a try. *So*, I thought, *let the dating game begin.*

"Hi, Jim, this is Lynne," I warbled into the phone. "I saw the ads you're running and feel you're someone special, someone I'd like to meet. I'm a widow who would eventually like to remarry and have a happy home for my two children. Please, please call." I'd hung up, then been seized with anxiety. Oh, *why* did I say that? I sounded so needy. I shouldn't have mentioned the kids. I even said the "M" word. He'll never call.

The next day at the office, the standard hassle continued. "Lynne, Mike and I are going skiing for a few days. Here's a list of things I need you to take over while I'm away," Melissa said as she left for lunch with the others.

By three in the afternoon, I was berserk with work.

Needing something to take my mind off the workplace, I called home to check my messages.

"Hi Lynne, this is Jim—the guy from the paper. I got your message. There was something in the way you said to 'please, please call' that got to me. You have such a sweet voice, and you sound honest. I'll call again later."

YES!

After three phone calls lasting long into the night, it seemed as though Jim and I had known each other for-ever. He even offered me references to prove he wasn't dangerous. Even so, I couldn't believe I agreed to a real date, but one of his calls had caught me off guard just as I was going out the door that morning.

I hadn't had time to change—didn't even have anything nice to wear. I was wearing jeans, having a bad hair day, and he was coming that evening.

At work, the usual rat race went on. "Hey, Lynne, I need these claims processed. You'll have to stay until they're finished."

"Oh, Cindy, I can't. Someone else will have to do them. I have a date tonight."

"You're going out? Who with?"

"A guy I met through a singles ad. He's picking me up at five."

She snickered. "Yeah, sure. If he shows up, I'll stay and do the reports."

At five-thirty, Cindy and Melissa were plastered to the office window, giggling and watching man after man pass by. Suddenly, Melissa peeled herself away and shrieked, "Lynne, I think your date's here."

I looked up, terrified. "A white Lincoln stretch limo?" I

forced a laugh. "That can't be for me. Must be for some executive going to the airport."

Not likely. The evil stepsisters and I were the only ones left in the building.

"That limo has to be for you. Go check it out. I want to see this Prince Charming. He must be a hoot," Cindy chortled.

"I cannot go out there. I'm not dressed for anything but a Happy Meal at McDonald's. I'm having an anxiety attack."

"If you don't go, I will. Mike's away. This guy could be a jerk, I suppose, but he's certainly a big spender."

That got me moving out the door and halfway across the sidewalk before I panicked. A limo! Me in jeans and frizz! I wanted to run—anywhere but there.

Too late. The door to the limo opened and my telephone dream date got out, smiling and holding two glasses of champagne! Behind me I heard Melissa shriek, "He's wearing a tux, and there's a violinist in the car!"

I couldn't believe what happened next. I absolutely freaked and planted a long, passionate kiss on him, spilling the champagne all over both of us. "Oh, no," I babbled. "I'm so sorry. I didn't mean—— I didn't think—"

"Don't apologize. I certainly have no complaints. There's more champagne in the car." He paused to take my hand. "Why are you shaking?"

"Why am I shaking? You've got a violinist playing the theme from *Romeo and Juliet*. Two women in my office have their nostrils flared against the office window. The last guy who showed any interest in me rode a Schwinn because he'd lost his license."

Jim chuckled, waved to Cindy and Melissa, and helped me into the limo.

Dinner was lobster and all the trimmings at the best seafood restaurant in town. He told me about *his* case of nerves that day and regaled me with stories of the terrible dates he'd suffered through. He was an excellent story-teller and a gentleman who was careful to avoid names and to take the blame for the disasters himself. He was as easy to talk to in person as he had been on the phone when he'd drawn me into telling him how challenging my life was. By dessert, we were laughing and holding hands. I even told him about the creepy neighbor who had stolen my bra off the line.

We had time for only one dance after dinner. I had to get home to my kids. He understood and told me to stop apologizing.

When Jim dropped me off, I stared out my window, watching the limo pull away. My heart was racing; I knew I wouldn't sleep that night. Then, I remembered who I was—a widow with two kids, a date in jeans and frizz with a nine o'clock curfew. He might be the kindest, most generous man I'd ever met, but he'd never call back.

The next morning, I arrived at the office feeling hung over from a lack of sleep and from regret. There they were, both evil stepsisters, by the water cooler. I figured when Jim didn't call back, I'd never hear the end of how I blew it.

"Lynne, I signed for this messenger-delivered goodie," Cindy said, placing the three-foot-long box on my desk.

Inside the box, surrounded by fresh orchids, was a two-foot-long, hand-constructed mini-clothesline, with a new

Victoria's Secret bra clothes-pinned to it, and a tiny spun glass slipper tied on with gold thread. The card said, "Cinderella, I believe you're missing one of these. I'd like to know if it fits."

JIM NOVOTNY

♥ *Chef Tips* ♥

1. During the dinner conversation will be something you can apply to a next-day Cinderella gift.
2. Take the next morning off from work and find something to remind her of the evening.

Kidnapped

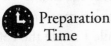 **Preparation Time**

Moderate

 Cost

$$$$

Chef

Male or Female

Planned spontaneity for couples whose busy lives don't offer many opportunities for spontaneity and privacy.

Ingredients

A Friday evening

A ruse to send your spouse to work without
　　his or her car

A bag packed with your necessities and a similar
　　bag for your spouse: toiletries, a big fluffy robe,
　　a favorite nighty

A "nest-building" box with candles, a tape
　　or CD player, and some romantic music

A babysitter

A hotel reservation

"*T*HE MARRIED CHASTE" someone has called those of us who, at a period in the almost-remembered past, had enough leisure time to fall in love, get married, and conceive children. Night after night my husband and I fall into bed exhausted, only to start another day the following day, part of the seemingly endless round of work, school, home-work, music lessons, sports events, doctor's appointments, and orthodontist's visits that define family life today.

I staggered out of bed that particular morning and leaned against the kitchen counter while I made the cof-fee. "There's got to be more to life than this," I said aloud to the coffeemaker. Then, as though I had heard someone else say it, I agreed. "You're right. You're absolutely right."

That was the beginning of the plot.

I called my neighbor Penny—I knew she would be staggering around her kitchen at that awful hour, too.

"Hey, it's me. Can you keep my kids for me tonight? After school and all night, until, oh, about noon tomor-row? Not an emergency. I have a plan. I'll call you later in the day and give you details. Thanks. Penny? Thanks a lot."

The kids were out the door and on the bus by the time Tim was out of the shower. I launched a trial balloon.

"My car is almost out of gas. I'll take you to work if I can keep the car. Okay?"

"Mmpnh."

I took that as an affirmative and threw on my favorite no-brainer outfit—black wool pants, a turtleneck, and a houndstooth blazer. In that outfit I become Wonder Woman in nothing flat. We were out the door in fifteen minutes.

I dropped him at work and arrived at my office early. I attacked my list of Things To Do with unusual energy because I was looking forward to my assignation with my totally innocent, unsuspecting husband. By 3:00 P.M. I was scooting out the door and hurrying home to execute the plan that had been taking shape all day.

I threw his toiletries and mine into a flight bag. I found my most glamorous black negligee and his cotton terry robe. Swimsuits in case there was a hot tub. No, on second thought, if there is a hot tub in the room, we don't need swimsuits and if there's not, forget it. A couple of candles, a boom box and some CDs, khakis, and a favorite sweater for him to wear home tomorrow. I traded in my houndstooth for a velvet blazer and I was set.

I was out of the house before the kids got off the bus. Penny would swoop them into her house, and they would count it an adventure.

I was waiting outside Tim's office building when he came out. He climbed into the car and, to his credit, noticed the velvet blazer.

"You look nice."

Maybe we weren't as far gone as I had thought.

We chatted through traffic until I pulled into the parking garage for the newest hotel in town.

"Dinner?" Tim asked. "What's the occasion?"

"The occasion, my dear, is that you have been kidnapped. You have been taken, without your permission, into foreign territory for immoral purposes. I didn't even leave a ransom note. You're mine."

"Should I struggle just to make it look good? So I can tell the police I put up a fight?"

"Struggle all you want. But follow me."

We held hands at the registration desk and giggled like newlyweds. Our room had a balcony overlooking the river and, *thank you, gods of hearth and home*, a hot tub.

Much, much later, we dressed and went to the dining room for dinner. We lingered over cappuccino and danced in the elevator on the way back to the room.

The next morning we opted for room service. "How profligate and slothful we are, heh, heh, heh," Tim chortled as he lifted the domed cover from the eggs Benedict.

I kissed the tip of his nose as I sat down across the tiny table from him. "The way I see it, Cassanova, it's cheaper than a divorce or psychiatric care. Besides, we can pay for it with the ransom money."

LYNN WHITED HUTTON

♥ *Chef Tips* ♥

1. Plan this on an evening your partner does not have work responsibilities (or tickets to the big game) the following day.

2. Arrange for overnight baby-sitting if necessary—swap out with a friend, and you keep her kids next Friday night!

5.

RECIPES THAT COST MORE THAN $160

A relationship should be sixty/forty.
Each person should give 60%
and expect to receive 40%.

— Frank Cabiroy

Helicopters & Horses

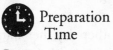 Preparation
Time

Fast

 Cost

$$$$$

Chef

Male or Female

*Opposites might attract, but love
is the glue that keeps them together.*

Ingredients:

Soft scarf

Assorted transport

Flowers

YOU KNOW the old saying: opposites attract.
Well, that's true and that's how it was for Janny
and me.

Janny's small and dainty and kind of old-fashioned; I'm
a mechanic and a center on the local football team.
She likes old things and Verdi's operas, red wine and roses.
I like motorbikes and sports, the Boss, and I've been
known to do a bit of hunting and fishing. She's got two
cats and I've got Mufti, my bitzer hound from the pound.
She's got this old-fashioned house and rambling garden,
and I've got an apartment over a garage.

We met by accident—literally. We bumped into each

other a few months ago, outside the antique shop she works in. We ended up having lunch together, and we've seen each other quite a few times since then. There are sparks between us, and I have a feeling this relationship could really go somewhere.

So when Janny looked at me the other day, her dark eyes doubtful, and said, "Do you really think this is going to work?" my heart sank to my boots. I know we're different, chalk and cheese in fact, but that doesn't worry me— I think we have a good thing going. She said she thinks so, too, but she's worried it won't last.

"We're as different as helicopters and horses," she said.

"Opposites attract," I reminded her.

"Mm. But sometimes it's just so they can crash into each other," she said.

"And sometimes it's so they can connect. Like us," I said, but I could see she wasn't reassured. I decided we needed the perfect date, so she could see we complemented each other—not collided.

Helicopters and horses. . . hm. It only took a few phone calls to make my arrangements, and I made sure I remembered to order a dozen red roses. She's a traditional kind of girl, my Janny.

Then I drove to her house and asked her to trust me. I tied a soft scarf around her eyes and led her to my pick-up. I knew where we were going, but I drove around in circles for a while, just to make sure she didn't have a clue where we were. Once we reached our destination, I led her to our waiting transport.

You should have seen her face when I took off the scarf. It's not every day a girl gets to go for a ride in a helicopter.

She protested a little, but I said, "C'mon, you can be a high flyer just for a few minutes," and she grinned and hopped aboard.

Man, I love flying. We rose straight up and skidded across the clouds, swooped through the blue, and floated down to the nearby Lake Park. After we'd alighted, the chopper took off and we were left in a quiet, sunlit haven. Tracks meandered through the reserve, trees clustered around the water, birds called in the distance, and some ducks paddled, serene and funny, toward us. Janny glowed. She'd never flown before and the color bloomed high in her cheeks.

She laughed and ran to the water's edge. "Brad, this is wonderful," she cried, but I wasn't finished yet, and a few minutes later a horse and carriage clopped into view. White horse and black shiny carriage, just like I'd ordered.

The driver saluted us, and I said, "Our transport, ma'am."

Janny looked from me, to the carriage, and back to me. A lot of different expressions warred on her face, but when I got the roses from the back seat and gave them to her, it was happiness that won. "Helicopters and horses," she said, and a grin tilted her wonderful, sensual mouth. "Best of both worlds, right?"

"We can have it," I said. "I can introduce you to my world, and you can introduce me to yours."

Janny nodded and looked around us, then back at me. "I'd like that," she said, and those simple words warmed me like the sun.

It was a great trip home. Slow and settled, clopping

along quiet back roads, and Janny and me, well, we discovered that we might be opposites, but we've got plenty in common, too.

SUE EMMS

💜 *Chef Tips* 💜

1. This recipe works well with any form of transport (tandem bikes, trains, boats, roller skates etc.) and any destination (the zoo, movies, amusement park). Let your imagination run wild.
2. Try an evening trip for added mystery.
3. Add a picnic basket for a great final touch.

East Meets West: A Double Date Surprise

 **Preparation Time**
Moderate

 Cost
$$$$$

Chef
Male or Female

A willingness to take chances and combine unusual
ingredients can lead to unexpected rewards.
Parental supervision may be advised.

Ingredients

1 man and woman from different cultures

1 set of traditional parents

1 restaurant (or other romantic locale)

1 birthday/anniversary cake

1 set of plane tickets

1 accomplice

SOME OF THE BEST SURPRISES in life come from mixing the most unlikely ingredients. People may warn that it will never work, but those who stubbornly persist—despite the risk of failure—are often rewarded with delightful combinations: peanut butter and chocolate, hot and sour soup . . . Rashida and me.

I first met Rashida, a petite, dark-haired, and lovely Indonesian woman, on a tennis court several years ago. A simple-hearted American with an uncomplicated view of romance, I didn't understand the implications when Rashida said she was Muslim. All I knew was that the moment our eyes first met, a quiet but unquenchable fire had been lit. As tennis games led to conversation, coffee, quiet walks around the lake, and dinner, cultural differences were soon consumed by a rising flame.

Eventually, however, it became clear that Rashida and I were two unlikely ingredients, a combination that promised as much risk of failure as it did reward. The realization hit me hard one night, just as our passionate embraces promised to bring us ever closer.

Suddenly there were tears in Rashida's eyes. She pushed me back, struggling to hold her own passions in check. "We can't do this."

I was confused. "What do you mean? We *are* doing this." By "this," I meant everything we had shared since we'd met: our lives, our dreams, our affections. I was ready to share more, a life-long commitment, and I thought she was, too.

But as we talked that night and continued to struggle over this issue for the months that followed, I slowly came to understand what she meant. While Rashida was educated in Western schools and had developed an open mind and broad tastes, her parents were raised in a strict Muslim culture. To them, certain ingredients were not meant to *ever* come together.

"I'm willing to convert," I protested. "I'll do anything to be with you, and I'll put my heart in it."

Rashida was touched, but unconvinced. "It's not that simple. Even Muslim men and women don't just meet on their own and marry. Matches have to be arranged by the parents and family."

I knew she was right. Despite our closeness, Rashida hadn't even told her parents about us, so great was her fear of disapproval. I tried every line of reasoning. Wasn't our love worth risking the consequences? But having been sent to private schools for much of her life, Rashida had already suffered years of painful separation from her parents. Even now, they lived far apart—Rashida's father and mother worked in San Francisco, while Rashida and I lived in New York City— and were lucky to see each other once a year. They missed each other very much. If anything, she wanted to be even closer to them.

I agonized over this stalemate for months, until finally it hit me. I may have won Rashida's heart, but the courtship wasn't over. Some ingredients were still missing. And that's when I began to make plans for a special date—not just Rashida and me, but a double date with an unusual combination. My plan centered around the fact that Rashida's birthday was coming up in a few weeks and that her parents' anniversary happened to be in the same month. Not the same day, but close enough.

Planning the surprise for Rashida was the easy part. "Just you and me at our favorite restaurant," I lied. "Candlelight, music, and maybe a surprise or two."

"A surprise?"

"A surprise or *two*," I emphasized, but refused to elaborate further.

Working the other half of the date was trickier. I spoke to Rashida's sister, and together we came up with a scheme. Then I called her father, identified myself as a real estate developer, and invited him to a special seminar, a rare business opportunity that he and his wife should attend. All expenses paid. On my recommendation, they called Rashida's sister, who backed up my story. A few minutes later, they called back and took the bait. The only near-hitch came when they learned that the seminar was in the same city Rashida lived in. They tried to insist on arranging a visit. I had to do some fast talking, explaining that the plane ticket restrictions required that they return right after the seminar. Finally, all the pieces were in place.

On the evening of Rashida's birthday, I called her and explained that there had been an emergency at work. I couldn't pick her up, but would meet her at the restaurant. Then, dressed in my best suit and tie, I met her parents at the airport and introduced myself as a representative for a land developers association. I even had brochures from a real agency for them to look at during the drive back.

When we arrived at the restaurant, my heart was pounding. I explained that the seminar was being held in a conference facility adjoining the restaurant. As we entered, I saw Rashida, seated at a table in a distant corner. Candles were lit and glowing on the white linen tablecloths, and a pianist was playing soft jazz. I worked my way across the room, Rashida' parents following me, completely unsuspecting.

Rashida looked up and started to smile. Then her expression froze, and her face literally went white. I glanced behind me and saw her parents' similar expressions. I barely had time to say "Happy Birthday" and "Happy Anniversary," before I was nearly knocked over amid the rush of hugs, cries, and tears.

When things settled down a few minutes later, I filled

everyone in on the scheme. To avert any suspicion, I quickly explained to her parents that this was my gift to Rashida for being a good "friend" and a great tennis partner. Then I excused myself, saying that the night was for family. But as I hoped would happen, Rashida's parents insisted I join them for the evening. I thanked them and seated myself a respectful distance from Rashida.

Initially, I stayed in the background and let Rashida and her parents catch up on recent events. But I soon joined in the laughter as they reminisced over past birthday parties and anniversaries, and at one point had a phone brought over so they could call Rashida's sister and let her join in the fun. My final surprise came near the end of the night when the anniversary/birthday cake I had ordered arrived, an Indian specialty dessert that I knew had sentimental meaning to the family. I was touched when Rashida's parents, seeing the cake, held each other's hands. By the end of the night, as the events of the evening began to hit home, I noticed Rashida's mother giving me several sidelong glances of curiosity.

When we left the restaurant, both parents thanked me sincerely and then spontaneously gave me a warm hug. Rashida continued to keep a polite but friendly distance from me, as she had all night, but when her parents actually teased her—"Aren't you even going to thank your friend for such a nice evening?"—she came over and also gave me a hug. As Rashida and her parents said goodbye and walked away together into the night, I'll never forget the knowing smile Rashida gave me as she turned back just before they were out of sight—nor how, a moment later, her mother did exactly the same.

The next day, after we waved goodbye to her parents at

the airport gate and they were safely out of sight, Rashida gave me a much longer, harder hug. When she finally pulled away, there were tears in her eyes. "Those were best two surprises I've ever received," she said.

I held her hand as we headed to the parking lot. "This 'arrangement' worked out nicely," I agreed. "But do you think there will be . . . others?"

Rashida laughed and dabbed at her wet eyes with a tissue. "Let's hope."

I looked in her eyes and saw that something had melted. I thought I'd seen the same expression in her parents' eyes a few minutes earlier as they waved good bye. By the time we reached the car, I decided that I liked the way things were going. The balance was good; the combination promising. Four unlikely ingredients; one delightful result.

JON QUEIJO

♥ *Chef Tips* ♥

1. This international recipe can work for any cultural combination. The secret is to recognize—and be bold enough to combine—the right ingredients.

2. The occasion for the double date does not have to be a birthday or anniversary; any situation with sentiment for all parties concerned will succeed.

3. The locale and surprise dessert are flexible as well. With the right ingredients, this recipe is guaranteed to delight in virtually any setting.

4. Cost will vary with travel distance.

Typical Dinner and a Movie?
NOT!

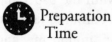

Preparation Time

Long

Cost

$$$$$

Chef

Male or Female

---

*Tired of that old accusation of being unimaginative?
Boring? Existing without a romantic bone in your
body? This date will change that notion and give
you a chance to show your favorite lady just
how romantic you can be.*

Ingredients

    Prepurchased tickets to a movie of her choice

    Small or medium sized boat, or a friend with one

    Bottle of Chianti

    Take-out dinner for two from a good Italian restaurant

    Table and two chairs

    CD Player and a couple of romantic CD selections

    *Several good friends, preferably those who owe you a
       favor or two*

I'M AN EARLY RISER, so every morning, for a number of years, the first stop in my day was the coffee shop down on Main Street. I'd get my coffee and my toasted raisin-cinnamon bagel and settle in to peruse the newspaper. I didn't give anything much thought at that time of day, really. When I was done with the paper and almost through with my coffee, I'd look around, listen to the bits and pieces of chatter going on around me, and watch people come and go. Every now and then, someone would catch my eye, or my ear. That's how I met Cathy.

I'd just folded up the paper and picked up my coffee cup when I heard a single voice through all the others.

". . . I know. I've met some really nice guys, but none of them have any imagination when it comes to a date. It's always dinner and a movie, dinner and a movie. I mean, it's a nice night out, but does it always have to be the same thing?"

I put down my cup and moved around in my chair in an attempt to locate the owner of the understandable complaint. I smiled. Now, who would be so thoughtless and predictable? Sounds like someone in a real rut, I thought. As I looked around as nonchalantly as I could, I heard the voice again.

"Well, I don't think Mr. Right exists, and if I get an offer for dinner and a movie this weekend, I think I'll just stay home and do my nails."

I located the voice and her friend, about ten feet from me—two women just getting up from their table. I didn't know which woman had made the comment, but I knew which woman had caught my eye. I'm sure I stared, but she didn't notice. Right then, I decided I was going to make it my business to get to know her.

She didn't show up for coffee again until the following week, but when she arrived, I was on my second cup of coffee and waiting for her. As she shifted her briefcase from one hand to the other, I asked if I could help. She flashed me a smile that made my heart skip a beat and then, suddenly, we were having coffee together, twice a week.

Convinced that I could come up with a date that would dispel that nasty dinner-date stereotype, I put together a scheme to surprise her and, I hoped, win her heart. It involved calling in one favor and owing one, but after discussing my plan with a friend who is the head-waiter at a local Italian restaurant and a mutual friend of ours who plays classical guitar in the same establishment, I was ready to ask Cathy out.

It was all I could do to keep a straight face. "How about dinner and a movie on Friday?"

Her smile reflected in her crystal blue eyes. "That would be nice. What do you want to see? Sci-Fi or an action movie?"

"Why don't you pick?" I asked, hoping that her choice would be something romantic.

"How about *Titanic*?" she asked eagerly.

I grinned like a teenager. From what I'd heard, that was an ideal choice. "Great! I'll check out show times and get tickets in advance so we don't have to wait in line. Do you like Italian food?"

She nodded and I took down her address. "I'll call you and let you know what time I'll pick you up." She smiled and gathered up her things. I rushed off to my office to start coordinating my "dinner" date.

I carefully calculated the time that Cathy would get home from work and chose the five o'clock showing. At lunch, I ran over to Loews and picked up the tickets. Then I called Chris and asked him if his boat would be at the dock on Friday night. He had no plans, told me to use the "Nauti-Gal" if I was so inclined, and wished me luck with my girl. I called Joe, the guitarist, and told him we were on. Jack was already figuring out menu selections that would work well for takeout.

I watched The Weather Channel that night and got a great forecast and the time for sunset. The movie let out at eight o'clock, the drive to the bay was thirty minutes, and sunset would happen about eight forty-two. I was thrilled and a bit anxious, but I knew that Jack and Joe wouldn't let me down. Joe owed me, big time, for the two weekends that I'd helped him paint his house. Jack was talking about hiring someone to prepare a business plan, so I volunteered to take care of that for him. They both promised to stop by the boat and get everything set up by eight-thirty, but would have to leave by nine-thirty in order to get to work on time.

I excused myself from the movie about ten minutes from the end. I reached Jack on his cellular phone.

"Are we all set, Bud?"

He laughed and said something to Joe that I couldn't hear. "Of course we're all set. Will you relax?"

"Easy for you to say. I've had two cappuccinos and there's a lot at stake here. How's the weather? Did Joe bring the CD player and the CDs?"

"It's a gorgeous night out here. And yes, Joe brought everything he promised he'd bring. Now, quit doing the Nervous Nellie routine and go see the end of the movie. It's not very romantic to leave your date in the theater all by herself, you know."

His chuckle was infectious. I hung up and slipped back into the theater. I placed my arm around Cathy's shoulders and pulled her close.

"Good movie, huh?" I nuzzled her cheek.

She turned her tear-streaked face my way and smiled. "The best."

We left the theater and headed east. We'd traveled about fifteen minutes before she spoke.

"What are you up to, Frank?"

"Me? I'm not up to anything, Cath. We said dinner and a movie, right? I just thought we'd eat over by the bay."

"Really? I don't believe there's an Italian place over there."

I smiled and placed my hand on hers. "Trust me, okay? I know this great little open air place that'll treat you like royalty."

I squeezed her hand and she studied me carefully before she settled back in the seat and watched the miles fly by.

We arrived at the bay only moments before sunset. In all its midsummer splendor, the sun flamed on the horizon, seemingly reluctant to give up its duty of the day to the descending blue-black of the night sky. We held hands as we strolled down the wharf, awed by the beauty of the twilight and enjoying the cooler breezes of evening. Since we'd parked quite a distance from Chris's boat, it was several minutes before we spotted Joe and Jack.

"Frank, look at those two guys over there. They're in tuxedos."

I smiled down into her eyes. "Yeah, strange apparel for this location, huh?" She nodded. "Let's go take a look," I said casually, pulling her along with me.

When we got up to the boat, Jack stepped up and bowed deeply. "Party of two?" he asked.

Cathy looked at me and I nodded. I could see a smile tugging at her pretty mouth.

He beckoned us on to the boat. "Will this table do?" he asked as he pulled out Cathy's chair and signaled me to be seated. She looked around and smiled up at him.

"This is perfect, thank you."

I picked up the long-stemmed white rose that lay on the table and offered it to her. "I hope you approve of my choice in restaurants."

Her eyes twinkled. "I certainly do, Frank. This is absolutely wonderful."

Joe played his guitar while Jack poured us each a paper cup of Chianti. I raised my cup and saluted. "Here's to a lovely sunset, an even lovelier woman, and good friends." Joe deftly fingered a soft love ballad on his guitar. I ached to hold her in my arms. "May I have this dance, my lady?"

Carefully, we stepped away from the little table and moved together in the small space allowed. I asked Jack to serve our meals and, as he placed the steaming trays of linguine and tomato-basil sauce on the table, I pulled her close. Our dance floor was only a couple of square feet, but we didn't mind.

"Happy?" I murmured into her silky hair.

"Speechless. This is so thoughtful, Frank. No one could say you don't know how to be romantic."

I smiled and nodded to my friends, who stood watching as we swayed.

"Dinner is served, sir," Jack announced. He helped Cathy back to her seat and placed a napkin in her lap, then refilled our cups and stepped back. Joe began to play another song, this one from *La Traviata*. We ate our meals enjoying the lovely evening, the music, and the magic of the night. By the time we'd finished dinner, Joe and Jack were ready to leave. The CD player was perched on the edge of the dock, playing music specifically designed to move the heart.

"I thought they'd never leave," I groaned when I could no longer see the retreating backs of my two friends. I pulled her into my arms and, once again, we filled our tiny space with dance, holding each other close.

She sighed softly, and I realized it was time to present the gift I had hidden for her. I reached down under the storage seat and retrieved a deep blue velvet shawl that matched her sparkling eyes. As I wrapped it around her shoulders and she turned her smiling face to me, I knew that my princess was happy. I grazed her lips with a gentle kiss.

"I haven't told you just how special you are, Cath."

She pulled out of my arms and reached up to touch my face, a feathery caress that took my breath away. Her eyes glittered almost as brightly as the stars that twinkled in the midnight sky above us.

"Oh, but you have, Frank," she whispered as she kissed me softly. "And now, I do believe it's my turn . . . ."

FRANK CABIROY / NANCY QUATRANO

❤ *Chef Tips* ❤

1. Check the weather report. Fair weather is a must.
2. If you don't have a classical guitar-playing friend, you can hire a freelance musician for $20.00 to $30.00 per hour.
3. Be sure to share the sunset.
4. The movie has to be one of her choosing. You show thoughtfulness by purchasing your tickets ahead of time.
5. The waiter has an important role. He must cater to your every need and still be nearly invisible. If you don't have any friends who can serve as your waiter, you can hire a good caterer to prepare the food and to serve it, black tie. Note that this is a replacement ingredient and will increase your costs somewhat.
6. Be sure to communicate with your "helpers," so that the timing is right for setting everything up. Double check the time that your date gets in from work, and allow a little extra if you are dealing with a high volume traffic area.
7. If you don't have a boat available, a cabin in the woods or a gazebo in a park setting would work also. Again, this would be a substitute ingredient and could potentially add to the cost associated with this recipe.

*Throw your heart into romance
and love will often follow.*

— Frank Cabiroy

About the Author

FRANK CABIROY is the author of 14 books, which have accounted for almost one million dollars in sales. As an entrepreneur, businessman, and computer professional, Frank has held various positions including president, director, manager, and instructor. A native of New York who lives in Virginia, he now pursues creative opportunities and travels the world. His success is due to hard work, perseverance, and a can-do attitude. He continually puts into practice his belief that people can achieve their highest goals through the power of positive thinking.

About the Editor

ANNE WALRADT holds a B.A. from the University of Idaho and an M.A. from Oregon State University. She has taught literature and writing on secondary and college levels, where she enjoyed prodding students into editing their own work toward perfection. She now lures prospective authors into workshops and urges them toward publication. Her workshops are held in the Northeast at romance writers meetings and conferences; the International Women's Writing Guild (www.iwwg.com) hosts her "Writing Down the FunnyBones" workshop at Skidmore College. When not freelance editing or writing articles, she writes creative nonfiction as Anne Frazier, mostly to protect her family about whom she writes and to keep them from writing about her.

Contributors

*M*ANY OF THE STORIES were contributed by readers like you, who were inspired to submit a story out of their life's experience. Some are existing and upcoming professionals that can be contacted at the addresses provided or through Pisces Press Publishing Company.

COLLEEN H. ADMIRAND is a full-time mother, part-time secretary, and an aspiring writer. She has written two contemporary romances, three short stories, a time-travel, and her WIP is a medieval trilogy. She is very active in NJRW and RWA. You can e-mail her at CHAdmirand@cs.com.

CAROLE DUNCAN BUCKMAN is a retired teacher and librarian. She is the author of *Signs and Wonders from our Journals*, a novel for young adults published by the St. Mary Press. She lives in Austin, Texas, with her husband, Bruce.

ROBERT S. COHEN is a writer, composer and producer. He has recently completed a book of short stories entitled *The Half-Life of Pizza and Other Slices* and the book and score for the Off-Broadway musicals *Suburb* and *God In Concert (One Night Only)*. Bob can be reached at Frogmastr@aol.com.

LORRAINE COYLE is a member of Romance Writers of America. Presently working on a romance novel, she has published essays and short stories in the *Moncton Times-Transcript* and various anthologies. New projects and her plans to revise several book-length manuscripts assure her hunger to write will forever be fed.

SUE EMMS is a New Zealand author of short stories and recipe books. A romantic at heart, one of her favorite memories is of the time her husband mowed I LOVE YOU into the grass outside her window.

SANDY FERGUSON lives in New Jersey with her husband, two children, and an assortment of pets. She writes time-travel romance and has been an active member of New Jersey Romance Writers for six years.

ANNE FRAZIER is writing a series of "Bombeckian" essays for *On the Home Front*. Her alter ego, Anne Walradt (AWalradt@aol.com), is a free-lance editor and teacher. A member of RWA, NJRW, and IWWG, her articles and essays have appeared in such diverse publications as *Maine in Print* and *Romance Forever*.

LYNN WHITED HUTTON is an ordained United Methodist minister, and a free-lance author and editor. She writes a weekly column for a local newspaper, loves to travel, and never gets enough time to read. With her husband and two teenage daughters, Lynn lives in the country outside Knoxville, Tennessee.

ELIZABETH KEYS is a multi-award winning author actively pursuing publication in book-length romance fiction. She currently juggles careers as Assistant Vice President of a local bank, part-time grants consultant, and organizes a household filled with children and lots of love. E-mail: e2keys@aol.com. *Thanks for the cookies and the story, Rita!*

SHARON L. KONSCHAK (sunnyk@imaginemail.com) is a poet and artist with credits in *Rewrites, Shared Vision,* and *Traveled Paths.* She recently started writing short stories and is working on a novel. When not writing, she is busy drawing and enjoying the meditative rewards of yoga.

PATRICIA LEARY, after earning BA and MA degrees from Rutgers University and enjoying careers in finance and management, reverted to the vocations of her childhood: bookworm and daydreamer: She has authored a variety of articles and columns, including "The Budget Romantic," and several not-yet-discovered romantic suspense novels.

HOLLY LOVE (hlove@ot.com) used her University of Pennsylvania degree to program computers before becoming a writer, editor, and wedding soloist. Her humorous and autobiographical essays appear in national newspapers and magazines, including the *Philadelphia Inquirer*, and in her *Main Line Times* column. She and pooch, Scooby, live in Havertown, PA.

RUTH MACLEAN is a full time writer of romantic fiction and a member of RWA and NJRW. Before writing took over her life, she was a nurse, a fashion commentator, and an accountant. Today, her life is filled with her writing, her children, her grandchildren, and her husband, Garry.

CHELLE MARTIN is a graduate of Monmouth University with a bachelor's degree in Business Administration / Marketing and a member of RWA and NJRW. A recent grand prizewinner in an on-line writing contest, she is currently working on several romance novels, a novella, and short stories. E-mail: TheHeroine@aol.com.

PENELOPE A. MARZEC, a member of the New Jersey Romance Writers and Faith, Hope, and Love, Inc., won first place in the 1998 Laurie contest with her manuscript, *Sea of Hope*. Her work has appeared in *Byline, Romantic Hearts, Writer's Digest, New Jersey Monthly, Today's Catholic Teacher*, and *The Asbury Park Press*.

MICHAEL MATTEO is the author of books, stage plays, magazine articles, and screenplays. Michael is a former public school teacher and presently owns a large costume and novelty business in Tampa, Florida. His latest screenplay, *Getting Personal*, is about a woman's search for her soul mate.

JAMES MITCHELL received a BA and an MFA from the American University in Washington, DC, and has worked as an editor, a translator, a filmmaker, a screenwriter, and a professor of film. He has published numerous stories and poems both in the States and in Europe. E-mail: cvocek@ex-pressnet.com or Kuba95@aol.com.

PATSY MOORE (patsyhmoore@juno.com) is a charter member of NOLA Chapter and national RWA. She has written feature articles, poetry, editorials, devotionals, and cocreated a cookbook. She's won prizes for romantic fiction, but isn't yet published in novels. She has judged in the Golden Heart, Golden Medallion, and NOLA's "Suzannah" Contest.

JIM NOVOTNY, president of MNR Communications Inc., is involved in publishing, entertainment, consumer, and medical advertising. He designed the Johnson & Johnson hospital packaging and the award-winning advertising campaigns for numerous corporations, currently for Baxter Pharmaceutical Products Inc. Contact at Suite 112, 120 Cedar Grove Lane, Somerset, NJ 08873.

MARIO I. OÑA attends the University of South Carolina (USC), majoring in Public Relations (PR). He freelances for several publications including USC's *The Gamecock*, Columbia's *The Free-Time*s, and the national magazine *Southern Business and Development*. He does extensive PR work for Capital Writer's Group PR Firm. E-mail: marioivan@aol.com.

LYN PALMER, married with two grown sons, resides in the scenic Columbia River Gorge area of Oregon. She works in a high school library with great students and staff and desires to meet Daniel Day-Lewis someday. "Make a Wish on the Moon" is her first published work.

NANCY QUATRANO has completed two full-length romantic suspense novels and three romantic suspense short stories. When she's not working as a technical writer for a paycheck, she's busy as mom, wife, and author. She can be reached on the Internet at weld1@bellatlantic.net.

JON QUEIJO is a medical writer who enjoys creative ventures into essay, fiction, and humor writing. While he has little experience in the art of cooking, he enjoys combinations of exotic ingredients that result in delightful surprises. He welcomes comments from those who wish to share similar recipes, at JonQueijo@aol.com.

KATHRYN QUICK, a member of NJRW, has been a stringer for newspapers reporting on local issues and penning a weekly opinion column called "A Quick Look Around." Outnumbered by men 4-1 at home, she discovered the Wide World of Sports. Kathye writes contemporary and historical romances and humor.

LESLIE ROGALSKI is a freelance writer and artist whose publication exposure includes *The Discovery Channel Online*, art and lifestyle magazines, and regional newspapers. Her short stories won prizes twice from *The National Writers Monthly*. Leslie leads writing workshops (K-12) and is a visiting author for The Pennsylvania Writing Project.

MARY STELLA is an aspiring romance novelist who loves writing about people and relationships. A native South Jerseyan, Mary is a freelance journalist, publicist, and marketing writer, whose work has appeared in various publications. She holds a degree in English from Monmouth University, West Long Branch, NJ.

GAIL WOODS THOMPSON is a published writer specializing in short and flash fiction. Gail is presently working on a collection of short stories. "After moving 30 times, I'm looking forward to sitting in one spot and revisiting, through my stories, all the unique and intriguing characters I've met along the way."

SEAN TONER is a 33-year-old novelist living in the Philadelphia area. He gives inspirational talks at area schools about prospering in spite of disability. He lost his sight in 1995 and hasn't been able to find it anywhere since. His E-mail address is zonk@snip.net. Hello Oprah.

Reader's Review

Romance Recipes for the Soul

We are interested in using comments from satisfied readers to tell others about this exciting book. May we share your views as written below with others?

_____

_____

_____

_____

_____

_____

_____

Yes, I agree that my comments may be used for national publicity and advertising. I understand that I will not receive any payment or compensation for this permission. My name or initials, as well as the city and state in which I reside, may also be used.

Signature: _____

Date: _____

Name: _____

City: _____

State/Zip: _____

Phone: _____

E-mail: _____

THANK YOU. Please return this form to:
Pisces Press Publishing Company
P.O. Box 3111 • Virginia Beach, VA 23454
Phone: (757) 721-2184 • Fax: (757) 721-7019
Web site: www.RomanceRecipes.com

Submit a Story

*W*OULD YOU LIKE to see your name in a future book?

Share your romantic heart with the rest of the world. If you have a story, poem, or article from your own experience or from someone else's that you feel belongs in a future volume of *Romance Recipes for the Soul*, please send it to us.

Frank Cabiroy
c/o Pisces Press Publishing Company
P.O. Box 3111 • Virginia Beach, VA 23454
Fax: (757) 721-7019 • E-mail: PPPco@aol.com
Web site: www.RomanceRecipes.com

We will make sure that the author is credited and compensated for the contribution.

Here's to Romance!

–Frank